A practical guide to survey research using SPSS®

Surveys with Confidence™

Mark Rodeghier

SPSS Inc.
444 N. Michigan Avenue
Chicago, Illinois 60611
Tel: (312) 329-2400
Fax: (312) 329-3668

SPSS Federal Systems (U.S.)
SPSS Asia Pacific Pte. Ltd.
SPSS Australasia Pty. Ltd
SPSS Benelux BV
SPSS Central and Eastern Europe
SPSS France SARL
SPSS Germany
SPSS Hellas SA
SPSS Hispanoportuguesa S.L.
SPSS India Private Ltd.
SPSS Israel Ltd.
SPSS Italia srl
SPSS Japan Inc.
SPSS Latin America
SPSS Middle East and Africa
SPSS Scandinavia AB
SPSS UK Ltd.

SPSS
Real Stats. Real Easy.℠

For more information about SPSS® software products, please write or call

Marketing Department
SPSS Inc.
444 North Michigan Avenue
Chicago, IL 60611
Tel: (312) 329-2400
Fax: (312) 329-3668

Preface

Surveys are omnipresent nowadays. We've all received numerous questionnaires in the mail, and most of us have been called for an interview. The quality of these surveys undoubtedly varies greatly, mainly because many people undertake the survey process with little or no formal training. Although surveys can be done by anyone who makes the effort, there is much existing knowledge that can be drawn upon to improve every step of the survey process. So, although you don't need formal training to be successful, some guidance is essential.

The purpose of this book is to provide you with the fundamentals of conducting surveys. It does so by summarizing information from many sources, including the real-life experiences of SPSS users in a wide variety of applications, to present concise discussions about and guidelines for every critical step in the survey process.

Surveys can generally be done either by interview or by what are generally termed self-administered questionnaires, usually sent by mail. This book emphasizes the latter, but much of its content applies equally to surveys done by interview. All of the chapters on data analysis will be helpful for any type of survey. Most of the chapter on data coding and cleaning can be used for interview data. Some of the information in the chapters on question writing and sampling also applies to interview-based surveys.

Also included is an appendix that lists several standard question formats for a variety of survey applications. Use them as written or modify them as necessary. Finally, an extensive bibliography is provided to supplement the text and suggest directions for further reading. Although this book is complete, an entire book could be (and has been) written about each chapter's topic, so eventually you'll want to broaden your survey knowledge.

The best way to learn how to do surveys is to try. Keep things simple in the beginning and seek out the advice of those knowledgeable about surveys, either in your organization or elsewhere. You will likely try some things that don't work, but don't be discouraged. As Thomas Edison realized, an unsuccessful experiment is not a failure, because you find out what doesn't work.

Acknowledgments

I want to thank Bob Gruen at SPSS, who suggested the idea for this book and helped carry it to fruition. I'm especially grateful to the many users of SPSS with whom I've discussed surveys and survey research over the years. Their comments and suggestions have contributed greatly to the practical information presented in the text. I'm grateful also to Don Faggiani, formerly of SPSS, who gave me my first opportunity to write about survey research. I also wish to thank the reviewers of this book, Shap Wolf and

Nancy Morrison, for their constructive suggestions. The editorial and production staff of SPSS was especially helpful with the many details of producing this book. Finally, as always, I wish to thank Kay Granath, my companion, for her continuing support of this book—and all of the other projects—that take me away from her and the cats.

Mark Rodeghier
Chicago, Illinois

Contacting SPSS Inc.

If you would like to be on our mailing list, contact one of our offices below. We will send you a copy of our newsletter and let you know about SPSS Inc. activities in your area.

SPSS Inc.
Chicago, Illinois, U.S.A.
Tel: 1.312.329.2400
Fax: 1.312.329.3668
Customer Service:
1.800.521.1337
Sales:
1.800.543.2185
sales@spss.com
Training:
1-800-543-6607
Technical Support:
1.312.329.3410
support@spss.com

SPSS Federal Systems
Arlington, Virginia, U.S.A.
Tel: 1.703.527.6777
Fax: 1.703.527.6866

SPSS Argentina srl
Buenos Aires, Argentina
Tel: +541.816.4086
Fax: +541.814.5030

SPSS Asia Pacific Pte. Ltd.
Singapore, Singapore
Tel: +65.3922.738
Fax: +65.3922.739

SPSS Australasia Pty. Ltd.
Sydney, Australia
Tel: +61.2.9954.5660
Fax: +61.2.9954.5616

SPSS Belgium
Heverlee, Belgium
Tel: +32.162.389.82
Fax: +32.1620.0888

SPSS Benelux BV
Gorinchem, The Netherlands
Tel: +31.183.636711
Fax: +31.183.635839

**SPSS Central and
Eastern Europe**
Woking, Surrey, U.K.
Tel: +44.(0)1483.719200
Fax: +44.(0)1483.719290

**SPSS East Mediterranea and
Africa**
Herzelia, Israel
Tel: +972.9.526700
Fax: +972.9.526715

SPSS France SARL
Boulogne, France
Tel: +33.1.4699.9670
Fax: +33.1.4684.0180

SPSS Germany
Munich, Germany
Tel: +49.89.4890740
Fax: +49.89.4483115

SPSS Hellas SA
Athens, Greece
Tel: +30.1.7251925
Fax: +30.1.7249124

**SPSS Hispanoportuguesa
S.L.**
Madrid, Spain
Tel: +34.1.443.3700
Fax: +34.1.448.6692

SPSS Ireland
Dublin, Ireland
Tel: +353.1.66.13788
Fax: +353.1.661.5200

SPSS Israel Ltd.
Herzlia, Israel
Tel: +972.9.526700
Fax: +972.9.526715

SPSS Italia srl
Bologna, Italy
Tel: +39.51.252573
Fax: +39.51.253285

SPSS Japan Inc.
Tokyo, Japan
Tel: +81.3.5474.0341
Fax: +81.3.5474.2678

SPSS Korea
Seoul, Korea
Tel: +82.2.552.9415
Fax: +82.2.539.0136

SPSS Latin America
Chicago, Illinois, U.S.A.
Tel: 1.312.494.3226
Fax: 1.312. 494.3227

SPSS Malaysia Sdn Bhd
Selangor, Malaysia
Tel: +603.704.5877
Fax: +603.704.5790

SPSS Mexico SA de CV
Mexico DF, Mexico
Tel: +52.5.575.3091
Fax: +52.5.575.3094

**SPSS Middle East and
South Asia**
Dubai, UAE
Tel: +971.4.525536
Fax: +971.4.524669

SPSS Scandinavia AB
Stockholm, Sweden
Tel: +46.8.102610
Fax: +46.8.102550

SPSS Schweiz AG
Zurich, Switzerland
Tel: +41.1.201.0930
Fax: +41.1.201.0921

SPSS Singapore Pte. Ltd.
Singapore, Singapore
Tel: +65.2991238
Fax: +65.2990849

SPSS UK Ltd.
Woking, Surrey, U.K.
Tel: +44.1483.719200
Fax: +44.1483.719290

Contents

1

Overview of the Survey Process

Surveys are used today to collect data on almost every conceivable subject, including attitudes about presidential candidates, television viewing habits, or the health and well-being of the populace. Information from surveys is used by the government to estimate critical economic data, including the unemployment rate, while businesses of all sizes increasingly rely on surveys to discover how to better satisfy their customers.

There are numerous ways to collect information about the world, with surveys being but one approach. Surveys are useful if:

- You plan to collect information by asking people questions in a standardized format.

- You can't contact the total population of interest (whether customers, members of an association, or all eligible voters), usually because that population is simply too large or it is too costly to do so, yet you do want to generalize results to that population in a rigorous fashion.

- It will be difficult to collect this information and generalize results by any other method, such as direct observation, experiment, or case study.

The two most important features of a well-designed survey are the use of probability sampling and the collection of standardized information. A well-drawn sample allows you to generalize results to the complete population and estimate the amount of error in the data. Writing thoughtful, well-conceived questions and administering them in a standardized manner ensures valid and reliable data that allow for analysis and generalization.

A census, on the other hand, allows you to collect data about all members of a target population and is often used in employee satisfaction studies, in customer satisfaction studies where the customer base is small, or, at the other extreme, in the U. S. census, conducted every 10 years to collect basic information about all Americans. However, because of nonresponse, use of a census does not guarantee that information will be collected about all members of a group. As a result of nonresponse, the data actually constitute a sample of the population, and generalizations will have to be made back to the full population.

Despite a carefully defined sample, many surveys flounder because of poorly designed questions. Many experienced survey researchers consider the writing of good questions to be the single most critical step in the survey process. A poorly drawn sample restricts your ability to generalize the results beyond the immediate sample, but poor questions can make even the data suspect, often to such an extent that you can't be certain exactly what a particular question is measuring. Such a situation presents a problem, but it may not be insurmountable. Only in the worst cases will the whole survey have to be redone.

Doing It Yourself

Many people and organizations are conducting surveys today, some of them very effectively. On the other hand, some people plunge ahead without fully understanding the principles of good survey design.

Survey research is a form of social science investigation, which may seem daunting. In some respects it is, but the fundamentals of good survey design are not hard to understand or apply, as long as you make the effort. These fundamentals have been refined through more than 50 years of study of survey characteristics by a diverse group of academics, market researchers, psychologists, and others. This text presents those basics.

Although a survey should be as scientific as possible, only the selection of a probability sample (to be defined in Chapter 3) and the estimates of error based on such a sample are capable of precise and rigorous definition. Just about everything else in a survey has some component of art in addition to the science involved. By that, we mean that there is no one correct way to accomplish a specific task and no principles that necessarily apply in every situation. How to go about getting a high response rate, what a cover letter should say, how to pretest the questionnaire, or exactly how to word a question will all vary from one survey to another. You will find plenty of research in these areas to guide you.

This leaves you, the survey researcher, plenty of leeway in how to meet the goals of your study. Fortunately, although each survey is unique, there are many principles that can apply to most circumstances. These principles allow a novice to conduct successful surveys, especially if the "98–2" rule is followed: Doing good work is 98% perspiration, 2% inspiration. Attention to detail is the survey researcher's credo.

There is an additional point that should be emphasized. All surveys have some weaknesses; even the U. S. census has shortcomings, as evidenced by the debate about whether inner-city populations have been completely counted. It is important, however, to recognize where your survey falls short and take that into account when reporting on the survey findings.

The Survey Process

Successful survey design must incorporate the following key stages:

Defining the Survey Objectives. You probably already have a pretty good idea of what you'd like to learn from a survey, but often the goals must be precisely defined to act as a basis for the writing of questions and, later, for the analysis and reporting of results. It isn't sufficient for a hospital administrator to have a general goal of "learning how satisfied our patients are with treatment and services." Instead, specific objectives should be listed:

- Determine the level of satisfaction with billing, food services, medical treatment, and discharge procedures by using at least two questions for each of these areas.
- Determine the level and quality of treatment and service that patients expect in these same areas.
- Identify specific problems encountered by patients and find out whether those problems were resolved.
- Gather demographic data (age, sex, race, income level, number of previous admissions) to allow comparisons across these subgroups and identify which patients are most satisfied (and most dissatisfied).

The definition of survey objectives is normally a collaborative project involving many people in an organization. This is both a strength and a weakness. Involving colleagues from throughout your organization will supplement your own thinking and increase their commitment to the survey and its results. Often, however, you are bombarded with ideas about what items should be included on a questionnaire and what information should be collected, so that including all of these suggestions might result in an unnecessarily long questionnaire.

The important point is that defining clear and reasonable objectives will give you a reference point at all stages in the survey process. Then, when making specific design decisions, you can always ask yourself, What should I do here to meet the objectives of this survey?

Choosing a Method of Data Collection. In this book, we will concentrate on surveys done by mail, although most of the guidelines discussed will apply equally to all self-administered questionnaires, such as those handed out at shopping malls or placed in employee mailboxes. The other common method of data collection is to conduct an interview, either in person or by telephone. Surveys are now also being done by fax, diskette, or even e-mail.

Selecting the Sample. Unless you plan to contact everyone in the population, you will need to decide who to contact. The key is to use appropriate techniques so that you draw a sample that allows for statistical inference and generalization back to the population. If you have a list from which to sample, your task will be simplified. If not, you will have to develop a sampling scheme.

After you choose a sampling method, there is still the question of sample size. There are both sophisticated and relatively simple means to choose an appropriate number of people to contact, but often the more sophisticated methods are not necessary for typical applications. Also, the budget for your survey may affect the size of the sample you choose, although mail surveys tend to be less costly than those done by interview.

Writing Questions and Designing the Questionnaire. These tasks are often perceived as the most intellectually stimulating in the survey process, except for the actual analysis of the data. You begin with a blank slate and try to construct valid and reliable questions, and then design a questionnaire that is aesthetically pleasing and holds the attention of the potential respondent.

We will discuss rules for writing questions and provide examples of question types for various common situations. You can supplement this advice by obtaining samples of questionnaires that have been used by others in your industry or field, or on national surveys. Learning what others have done is very helpful, if only to illustrate what not to do.

Designing the format of a questionnaire is truly an art, particularly if you use powerful desktop publishing software to create the document. Although a little clip art can go a long way, the effort invested in creating an attractive questionnaire usually has a high payoff.

Don't neglect a pretest of the questions and questionnaire. Regardless of how insightful and comprehensive your questions seem, trying them out first on an actual respondent, before spending thousands of dollars at the printer, is good survey practice.

Collecting the Data. This is the most tedious phase of the process and involves strict attention to detail. Your goal must be to get a completed questionnaire from as many people in the sample as possible. The tasks include distributing the questionnaire, maintaining a database of responders and nonresponders, and sending out reminders. If you mailed one letter, you can mail a thousand (along with reminder postcards and replacement surveys).

Timing is critical in this phase. You may have to produce a report based on the survey soon after the data are collected, and the sheer number of tasks to be completed make teamwork and coordination crucial.

Coding and Cleaning the Data. Once the last survey has trickled in (actually, they may continue coming in for months, so you typically have to set a cutoff date), the data must be entered into a database for analysis. Chapter 4 discusses several options for data entry, including SPSS.

Coding the data usually involves more than just taking a response from a survey and mechanically entering it into a software application. Judgment is often required, and you may need to create a special coding scheme for open-ended questions, unless you plan to enter responses exactly as written.

Once the database is created, you need to check for data entry errors, an easy task to perform in SPSS. Unlike earlier phases of the survey process that take some time for development (questionnaire design) or execution (data collection), data coding and cleaning can proceed rapidly if enough resources are devoted to the work.

Examining the Data. Before analysis can begin, you should look at the distribution of responses for all of the items, searching for impossible responses, items with little variation, or items that need to be recoded into a fewer number of responses. Use of various graphical techniques can be helpful as well.

Analyzing the Data and Creating Reports. This step is the payoff for all the work you've done in the previous steps. The analysis can be as simple, or complex, as the demands of the study require. SPSS provides a full set of statistical procedures and graphical techniques that are appropriate for all types of survey data. We will mention resource limitations in subsequent chapters when they might affect the survey process.

Available Resources

Money, personnel, and time are not unlimited, so you will have to balance these constraints when planning a survey. For example, since examining the data is normally done by one person and doesn't cost too much in time or money, it must always be done in every well-conducted survey. Conversely, sending an additional questionnaire to those in the sample who haven't responded is costly and time consuming and so may or may not be done, based on cost alone. We will discuss resource limitations in more detail when they might have an impact on the survey process.

If resources are limited, don't scrimp on the efforts devoted to obtaining a high response rate. Low response rates are the bane of mail surveys, and low enough rates can negate the good work done in the other phases of the survey process.

Record Keeping

We have to keep many records in our daily life, whether for personal, business, or tax purposes. Keeping complete records of the survey design and data collection process is crucial because it enables you to:

- Reconstruct and review all decisions, include this information in reports and presentations, and answer questions about what was done and why.
- Review the survey design process to correct mistakes, note what went well, and apply these lessons to your next survey.
- Estimate and report on the amount of resources spent on each phase of the survey.

To facilitate thorough project assessment and reporting, choose a software program that will allow you to easily record and track all relevant information about the survey process.

Creating a Time Line

The general stages in the survey process discussed above consist of many tasks that have to be completed to actually "design a questionnaire" or "collect the data." Your survey project will run more smoothly and you'll be better prepared to cope with unexpected problems if you create a time line that details the specific tasks (with time estimates for each) necessary to complete each stage. For example, the preparation of the questionnaire involves designing and laying it out, informal and formal pretesting, incorporating modifications, creating a final product, and, finally, the printing.

As noted earlier, many tasks are done simultaneously in a survey, particularly the selection of a sample and creation of the questions and questionnaire. A time line will help you manage the two (or more) things that you need to do at the same time to finish the survey within a reasonable time frame.

Surveys done by mail take longer, on the average, than other forms of data collection, and you will need to take this into account when planning the work. It is impossible to provide specific guidelines for the amount of time it takes to complete some phases of the survey process, such as question development. However, mailing the questionnaire, waiting for returns, and sending reminders always takes more than a month and can take even longer if you send additional reminders. More specific advice will be provided in the following chapters.

How SPSS Helps You in the Survey Process

SPSS is a powerful statistical analysis and reporting program. It also includes the Data Editor window, which provides a convenient, spreadsheet-like method for defining variables and entering data. However, SPSS cannot assist you in creating a sample (unless your population is already stored as an SPSS data file) or in writing cogent questions and designing attractive questionnaires. Nor can SPSS help you manage the data collection process, merge mailing lists, or create labels; other software can be used to accomplish those tasks.

SPSS can, however, be used to record survey responses. And once the data have been collected, SPSS will be the foundation for all remaining steps in the survey process, from data coding and cleaning through reporting and analysis. We will illustrate how SPSS can accomplish these various tasks with concrete examples and step-by-step instructions.

Other Sources

This text is reasonably comprehensive and covers the fundamentals of survey research. However, as you progress and increase your expertise, you'll want to review other sources for survey research advice and examples. The bibliography contains extensive references, organized by topic, that cover all aspects of the survey process.

Data for Examples

In this book, examples are based on a survey done for the Personal Electronic Products (PEP) company. The data are real, although the organization's name has been changed. The company sells consumer electronic products to customers in the United States and abroad. The survey used here was mailed only to customers in the United States. In this study, PEP contacted customers who owned a fax machine or personal photocopier. Sample selection was done from the existing customer database, which is based on registration records. PEP was interested in gathering more demographic information about their customers, determining the level of satisfaction with these two products, finding which customers were more (or less) satisfied, and learning what types of problems customers had encountered.

2 Writing Questions and Developing Questionnaires

We begin our review of survey elements with the writing of questions, the central focus of any survey. When survey research began over fifty years ago, very little was known about how to write effective questions. Unlike sampling, a technique developed mathematically and precisely, learning how to construct useful questions was very much a trial-and-error process until the 1960's, when more work was devoted to this area. As a result, practical guidelines have evolved that apply to most surveys.

Only someone familiar with an organization and its customers, clients, and/or employees can write penetrating questions that will elicit the information sought. However, knowledge of an organization and its information needs is not a guarantee of success. Although you don't need professional help to write good questions, it is easy to write poor questions unless you are careful. The guidelines discussed in this chapter will help you analyze your target audience and focus and refine your questions.

Much of the information in this chapter is prescriptive in nature, listing rules and guidelines, often without further elaboration. See the bibliography when you want to explore a topic further. See the appendix for many examples of successful question types for a variety of situations.

General Principles

Keep these two guiding principles in mind as you write questions and develop a questionnaire:

- Make the respondent's task as easy and simple as possible.
- Try to keep the respondent's interest level and attention at a maximum with interesting questions and well-designed questionnaires.

Additional, more specific guidelines include:

- When in doubt, write fewer questions rather than more.

- Make questions as short and clear as possible. A maximum of 20–25 words is a reasonable goal.
- Don't ask for information unless you can imagine how it will be used to meet the goals of the study. Avoid going on fishing expeditions for data.
- Get your questions on paper as soon as possible and try them out, before any formal pretest, on colleagues, friends, and, if possible, people from the target population. In general, the more feedback on questions and the questionnaire, the better.
- As much as possible, use questions from preexisting surveys. See the bibliography for a list of sources, and use surveys in your industry or field as models. (Of course, avoid copyrighted instruments, or get permisison to use them.)

All question writing rules can be broken if you have a *good* reason to do so. Specifically, rules can be broken because of special characteristics of the respondents or particular goals of the survey. If your population is well-educated (for example, university professors), you can probably write somewhat longer, more complex questions. However, with longer questions, you run the risk of lowering response rates, always a serious concern for mail or self-administered surveys. And even university professors are likely to appreciate short, concise questions.

Organizing the Task

Developing a questionnaire can seem overwhelming when you first begin the task. Where should you begin? How should you begin? The following suggestions should ease the task.

To write effective questions, you first need a clear outline of the objectives and goals of the survey. The objectives should be stated as precisely as possible. For example, for a survey of outpatients at a medical center, one objective could be "Determine how efficiently administrative matters were handled from the patient's perspective, including parking, first contact, and procedures in the department where tests were done."

Items requiring respondents to recall information from memory are prone to error.

There are three general question objects: attitudes, behaviors, and characteristics of the respondent. Most surveys focus on attitudes and demographics, such as gender, age, and income. Behavior questions typically ask about the frequency with which a specific activity occurs, such as how often someone goes to the drug store or watches television. However, behavior questions, broadly defined, apply to a wide range of topics. To inquire about how efficiently outpatients are processed, we could ask the patients to estimate the amount of time between their arrival at the medical center and the beginning of their tests and procedures. Such a question addresses more directly the efficiency issue than simple opinion items (although perception is obviously an important factor as well).

Further organize the questionnaire by breaking it into sections and specifying an approximate number of questions for each section. A bank might want to ask its customers to evaluate teller services, ATM usage, and other, more specialized, services. Also of interest would be problems encountered, overall customer satisfaction, and a demographic profile. Each area of investigation would become a section of the questionnaire, each with its own objectives.

For surveys done by telephone, plan no more than 15 minutes, preferably 10 minutes, per interview.

You should also have a firm idea of what the length of the questionnaire will be. Because of varying font size, the amount of white space, and design elements, no hard and fast recommendation can be made for the maximum number of questions on a self-administered survey. Nevertheless, a length of one to four pages is highly recommended. You should have the number of pages in mind when developing the outline of questions and sections.

Response Options

Questions consist of more than just carefully crafted sentences. They must also allow for a response, either by providing structured response options or by allowing for an open-ended response. Response options can be classified into many schemes, but perhaps the most crucial (because it relates to data analysis) is whether responses are on a nominal, ordinal, interval, or ratio scale.

- **Nominal** scales merely assign values to categories of a variable, but the categories can't be ranked, and the numbers assigned have no intrinsic meaning. A question asking for place of residence in the United States by region—East, Midwest, and so on—is gathering nominal data, since regions can't be ranked and have no intrinsic numeric value.

- **Ordinal** scales assign numeric values to categories that correspond to the rank of the categories on some underlying variable or construct. Asking whether a respondent would recommend a hotel to others, with response choices of *Would definitely recommend*, *Might recommend*, and *Would definitely not recommend* collects ordinal data. The answers can be ranked from high to low on the variable or factor of "willingness to recommend this hotel." However, the distance between the first and second categories is not necessarily equivalent to the distance between the second and third categories.

Technically, income is measured on a ratio scale, since it has a true zero point. We won't be concerned with this distinction.

- **Interval** scales have the properties of ordinal scales, plus the additional characteristic that a given interval on the scale corresponds to the same amount of what is being measured. Income measured in dollars is on an interval scale, since the difference between $20,000 and $30,000 dollars is the same as that between $90,000 and $100,000.

To select an appropriate analytical technique in SPSS, you must know on what scale a variable is measured. Most survey data are best measured on either a nominal or ordinal scale; these items are **categorical**. For certain questions, you will have no choice but to use a nominal or ordinal scale. Gender, ethnicity, and the type of service used or product owned by a customer are all naturally measured on a nominal scale. Attitude items asking for the rating or evaluation of various attributes and characteristics of a product, service, or organization are most naturally measured on an ordinal scale, from a less favorable to more favorable rating.

When you write questions using categorical response choices, the response alternatives must be exhaustive and mutually exclusive. All possible response choices must be listed or, if necessary, a separate "other" category included to allow for unanticipated responses. In addition, there can be no overlap of categories (such as coding age in groupings of 20–30 years and 30–40 years, which allows someone 30 years old to choose more than one category).

That survey data are most often categorical explains why crosstabulation—tables with the categories of one variable forming the rows and a second variable forming the columns—is the most common method of data analysis. On the other hand, much more powerful methods of analysis are available for data measured on an interval/ratio scale.

This fact leads to two common practices, the first of which is often misguided. First, inexperienced survey researchers often try to measure as many questions as possible on an interval/ratio scale. They may ask for exact income in dollars, the precise number of trips to a convenience store in the past month, or the exact airfare paid for a recent trip. These questions are not easy to answer unless records are consulted, and for the convenience store question, no records are available. You can avoid such problems by asking for numeric information on ordinal scales—for example, the number of trips to the convenience store can be measured in categories of 0, 1, 2, 3–4, 5–6, and 7 or more.

Second, both inexperienced and experienced survey researchers typically treat the 1 to 5 or 1 to 7 ordinal scale as interval/ratio data for purposes of analysis. This practice, done cautiously, is reasonably safe. Although a 1 to 7 scale most certainly does not have the properties of interval/ratio data, the advantages of being able to use techniques such as regression, analysis of variance and factor analysis are commonly thought to outweigh the distortion done to the data. However, in theory, ordinal scales should be analyzed with categorical data analysis techniques.

Yes/No Responses

Dichotomous items should not be used as dependent variables in regression or analysis of variance. For more information, see Chapter 10.

One special type of response option deserves a separate mention. Variables with two categories are usually thought of as nominal data. Common questions of this sort measure whether a respondent experienced any problems, whether a problem was resolved, or whether one would buy or use a product or service. A *Yes/No* response scale is a **dichotomous** scale and, interestingly, can be treated as either a nominal or ordinal scale. Asking whether problems have occurred is often a very effective predictor of overall satisfaction. Furthermore, in regression analysis or analysis of variance, dichotomous items can be used as predictors—in other words, as interval-scaled variables. So, for all of these reasons, the *Yes/No* question is a useful addition to your questionnaires.

Closed versus Open-Ended Questions

One of the most important decisions to make about almost any question is whether to offer any response choices at all. If not, the alternative is to provide a space for respondents to provide an unstructured response. These questions are **open-ended,** because you can't anticipate exactly how people will respond. Most experts on self-administered surveys suggest that you use open-ended questions as little as possible because of the following potential difficulties:

- Answers are more difficult to interpret and to code than closed formats and will, if nothing else, take longer to code, slowing down the survey process.

- The propensity to provide an open-ended response, and the length of response, are often related to respondent characteristics, chiefly education. This may bias the results.

- Coding of the answers can only be done properly with a well-developed theoretical scheme, especially when the codes are to be used in later analysis beyond simple reporting of the responses.

- Those who don't mention a certain topic simply may not have thought about it when answering the question but would have answered differently if presented with response choices.

Of course, many surveys do include open-ended questions, which may be useful if:

- The number and diversity of responses is unknown or too great to be listed and providing only a few categories might seriously bias the responses toward those choices (imagine an ice cream store asking for your favorite flavor of ice cream).

- You want to determine what ideas, thoughts, or concepts first come to mind when a specific question is posed.
- You use the question as a chance for the respondent to comment on anything not covered on the survey. (This type of open-ended question is often placed at the end of the questionnaire and should be included only if the comments will actually be reviewed.)

It has been our experience that managers often give more weight to responses to a few open-ended questions than to the answers to dozens of closed questions that have been analyzed statistically. Many people seem to prefer verbal over quantitative information. However, it is extremely rare for the critical findings from any survey to come from open-ended questions, so don't use or present them unless you are clear about the limitations of this form of response.

Writing Effective Questions

The general guidelines for writing effective questions have thus far emphasized the importance of writing neutral, clear questions and providing a well-defined response task for the respondent. As you begin to write questions, keep these additional suggestions in mind:

- If there is any chance that a term will be unclear or unknown to some respondents, provide a definition or clarification.
- Use simple language rather than less commonly used words or terms, and avoid slang and abbreviations.
- Avoid double negatives, compound sentences, and complex question formats.
- Avoid skips (an item that doesn't apply to all respondents) whenever possible. If you must include skips, provide clear instructions.
- Make sure that each question has only one topic (for example, don't ask in one question about problems customers have had using the ATM machine or interacting with tellers at a bank—these are two separate topics).
- Avoid loaded and leading questions (*Most doctors say that exercise is good for you. Do you agree?*).
- Avoid questions that ask why someone has a particular attitude or has engaged in certain behavior. Instead, ask specific questions that cover the range of reasons by using declarative sentences (*I bought the fax machine because of the reputation of the company.*).
- Avoid questions that ask respondents to rank choices. They are difficult to analyze unless sophisticated methods are used. If you do include such a question, limit the number of ranks to three. Alternatively, have respondents rate a series of objects, then rank order them yourself, using the ratings.

- When measuring the frequency of a specific behavior, avoid using verbal scales with choices like *Frequently*, *Often*, and *Sometimes*. Instead, ask for these data in grouped categories by frequency of occurrence. If you must use verbal scales, keep them the same from survey to survey so that you can compare results.

If you plan to conduct surveys of the same population on a regular basis, for the sake of comparability, try to modify questions as little as possible from one study to the next.

Scales

The most common response option in surveys is undoubtedly an ordinal scale of five or seven categories, with verbal labels to anchor the endpoints. These scales are commonly used to measure ratings, feelings, opinions, or other subjective states about almost anything, from politicians to breakfast cereal. The fact that scales are widely used does not make them an obvious choice for your own survey, but they certainly have a place in many questionnaires.

A **scale** is a ranked list of responses that runs from one pole to another (*Strongly disagree* to *Strongly agree*). The psychologist Rensis Likert was the first to study these scales in some depth, thus they are referred to as **Likert scales**.

If you use a scale, you must decide how many categories it should have. Considerations include the following:

- The larger the number of scale points, the more reasonable the use of general linear model techniques, such as regression.

- Scales of five points or more are reasonably **reliable**, which means that they consistently measure the object of the question.

- If respondents haven't thought much about an issue, providing a greater number of scale points may reduce reliability or, at the least, make the response task more difficult.

- Scales with three or four points make the use of general linear model techniques very questionable.

The above considerations lead to the following advice: Scales of five to seven points are perfectly adequate for most survey applications and are recommended. When in doubt, use fewer categories.

Should scales be listed on the questionnaire with the most positive end first or last? Research on this topic is not clear-cut, so the best advice is to pick one format and stick with it. (An exception to this rule is the reversal of response scales to discover inattentive respondents, discussed below.)

Including a Middle Alternative

Likert scales should almost always be balanced, with the same number of negative and positive categories. Another decision is whether a scale should contain a neutral category that is neither positive or negative. Scales with an odd number of points have a natural middle; scales with an even number of points do not.

Advice differs on the wisdom of including a middle alternative. Experiments have shown that, most of the time, offering such a choice understandably decreases the responses to the other categories but that the relative ranking of the categories is retained. Thus, the category chosen most often if there is no middle alternative will still be the one chosen most often when a middle choice is included, and so on.

Given this finding, our advice is to include a middle alternative, unless you have a good reason not to. Don't include such a category when you want to force respondents to make a positive or negative evaluation. For example, if you are asking about a sensitive matter, some people might prefer to take a stance between two extremes so as not to reveal their attitude. Nevertheless, if it makes sense for people to have a neutral or middle-of-the road opinion (as with political views), you should include a middle category.

Other Response Options

There can be no doubt that on many subjects people have little, if any, opinion. This criticism is often leveled at all survey research by those who believe that surveys force people to give opinions they didn't have before the question was posed. Just as bad, some survey researchers may use question formats that are artificial and can't readily be applied to the real world. Although there is some truth to these criticisms, especially for surveys done on foreign affairs and political issues, survey research can gather useful information, provided it is carefully done.

Fortunately, when you construct questions, it is likely that the respondents will be familiar with the topics of the survey. Businesses ask their customers about products or services they use, hospitals ask former patients about their care, and companies ask employees how well they like their jobs and company policies. In each of these situations, the respondents are familiar with the topic they are being asked to evaluate.

Still, not all questions will apply to everyone, and there will be items about which someone may legitimately claim to have no opinion (often because of limited use of a service or product, for example). In that case, you should probably offer an explicit response choice for the respondents who can't provide a valid answer. If you don't, you will be unable to differentiate between those who don't know and those who refuse to answer.

Not Applicable

If there is any chance that a question might not apply to every respondent, you should include a *Does not apply* or *Not applicable* response. *Not applicable* choices don't always require specific skip instructions. Consider a bank asking a series of *Yes/No* questions about characteristics of their ATM machine in the lobby. If one item reads *Were ATM deposit/payment envelopes available?*, a third choice, *Not applicable,* should be offered for those people who either brought an envelope with them or didn't need an envelope for their last transaction.

Don't Know

Unlike our advice for the *Not applicable* response, we generally recommend against including a *Don't know* option. The research on this matter clearly demonstrates that including a *Don't know* choice will reduce the number of valid responses and not significantly alter the relative distribution of responses in the other valid categories.

Surveys are plagued by missing data, most commonly caused by respondents simply skipping some items. Since a *Don't know* response is essentially missing data for purposes of analysis, providing this option makes data analysis more cumbersome. Second, if you ask respondents only about subjects on which they can reasonably be expected to have an opinion—and also provide a *Not applicable* category when appropriate—it is reasonable to press people to give an opinion rather than allow them an easy bailout by saying *Don't know*. A third, less critical reason not to include a *Don't know* option is that an extra category on each question clutters the questionnaire. As discussed in the sections on questionnaire design, a simple and uncluttered questionnaire will encourage respondents to answer the survey.

Exceptions to this advice include questions about future intentions (for example, which candidate someone plans to vote for) and the recall of past events.

Recalling Past Events

Asking about a respondent's behavior—items bought, number of visits to a medical center—requires the recall of past events. Because memory is not perfect, there is more chance for error with recall questions than with questions about current attitudes and opinions. Even so, many surveys require the collection of information that depends upon recall.

Recall questions are prone to two types of errors: forgetting and time-compression, or telescoping. Forgetting is a recognized problem and one to which we are all prone. The likelihood of forgetting becomes more pronounced as questions go back further in time or ask about unimportant events. Telescoping is not as well known or understood but is actually quite common. It refers to the tendency to remember events as occurring closer in time to the present, so that a question about events in the past three months may elicit responses based on events occurring within the past six months instead.

Since the recall of specific information is not flawless, one general strategy is to provide respondents with discrete categories as response alternatives rather than request an open-ended response. Thus, when inquiring about how often a customer visited a bank in the past month, provide categories from which to choose (0, 1, 2–3, etc.). It also helps to tell respondents to take their time when answering questions, although for self-administered questionnaires, there are presumably no time constraints. Telescoping is not so easy to overcome. The best strategy is to:

- Ask about behavior since an outstanding date, such as New Year's Day, or since a major event that all respondents will recognize. Mentioning a date seems to provide an anchor that reduces telescoping.

- When referring to time periods, always use specific units—*How many weeks since your last visit to our store?*—rather than *How long has it been since your last visit to our store?*

Since behavior data are subject to error, analysis should be done more cautiously than for of other kinds of data. This may mean using only techniques for ordinal, rather than interval, data analysis.

Demographics

Many surveys collect information on respondent age, gender, education level, income, length of time as a customer, place of residence, and so on. Include information of this sort only if it will further the objectives of your survey. Similarly, even if it's intriguing that one group likes your product or services more than another, if no action can be taken based on that difference, why bother collecting the information? As advised earlier in this chapter, collect only information relevant to the goals and objectives of the survey. If you don't need to know some-one's age, gender, or the like, don't ask. Or, as is becoming more common, make answering those questions optional. It will make the questionnaire shorter and just might lead to a higher response rate. Specific examples of demographic items are included, along with other question types, in the appendix.

Designing Questionnaires

A visually appealing, easy-to-complete questionnaire is just as important to the success of a survey as any other element. When you design a questionnaire for mail and self-administered surveys, keep these objectives in mind:

- You must motivate the respondent to begin the questionnaire.

- You must provide clear directions and an easy-to-use document to reduce error and motivate the respondent to complete and return the questionnaire.

Over time, Americans have become familiar with surveys and the specific features of questionnaires. The benefit of this familiarity is that respondents are better able to cope with poorly designed questionnaires. Even without specific instructions, respondents know that they are supposed to check a box, circle a number, or fill in a blank line. However, the proliferation of surveys has, over a number of years, led to declining response rates to all types of surveys. Since mail and self-administered surveys are prone to low response rates, a well-designed questionnaire may encourage response and so deserves considerable effort.

The power of the word processing and desktop publishing programs now available enable you to produce professional-looking questionnaires. You should exercise restraint in choosing fonts and decorative elements so that the appearance of the questionnaire will not detract from the content.

Design Guidelines

Questionnaire design has not been a hotbed of research, unlike the topic of how to write good questions, which has benefited from continuing attention. As a result, many areas of questionnaire design are relatively unexplored, so that on some issues there are no firm guidelines. Nevertheless, certain design principles have been found to work for a majority of surveys:

- Try to balance the amount of white space and text, but when in doubt, always leave more white space. Questionnaires should be uncluttered and easy to read.

For surveys conducted by interview, try to make the task easy for the interviewer. For example, separate instructions to the interviewer from questions he or she will read to the respondent.

- If you can, make the questionnaire into a booklet, preferably somewhat smaller than a standard sheet of paper. A smaller questionnaire seems less of a burden to complete, and a booklet has a more professional appearance.
- Choose a font that's easy to read, and choose a point size large enough for all respondents to read easily.
- Restrict the number of fonts used in the questionnaire to two.
- Provide instructions about how many boxes to check or items to circle. This is especially important if you are switching back and forth between single response and multiple response questions.
- Provide check boxes to mark or numbers to circle, rather than a blank line. A check box can take the form of a box, circle, parentheses, or brackets. (We tend to prefer a box.)
- Distinguish the questions from the response choices by using boldface for one and regular weight for the other, or by using upper case for the responses. Also, it's a good idea to use italics for directions to the respondents (for example, *Please check one box*).
- Print the questionnaire on both sides of the page.
- Enhance the cover of the questionnaire with some type of graphic.
- Unless the questionnaire is short, break the questions into logical sections by topic. Provide a section title indicating the change of topic.
- No particular paper color has been shown to produce higher response rates, but if you want to use something other than white, we recommend muted shades of gray or blue. Avoid bright colors unless you've pretested a questionnaire using them.
- If anonymity isn't an issue, place an identification number on each questionnaire. Hand-numbering machines are available to accomplish this task.
- If resources allow, you can use two colors, but don't use more than two.
- To save space, you can put two columns on a page. This works best when questions and responses are short.
- As a rule, don't place more than ten Likert-type items together, since too many can lead to respondent fatigue and inattention.
- If you have many sets of Likert-type items, there is the possibility that some people will begin marking the same answer all the way down the page—picking "4" on a five-point scale over and over. To counteract this, you can flip the scales (don't do so on the same page) so that some scales run from positive to negative, and others, the reverse. However, if you use this technique, you *must* supply very clear directions and note in them that the response scale has been reversed (the theory is that those not paying attention won't read the directions anyway).

- If you feel it will not distract the respondent, place code numbers—the actual numbers that will be entered in the data file—next to response choices. This will decrease error during data entry.
- Don't continue questions and response categories from one page to the next. Adjust the spacing between questions, or move questions around so that each question begins and ends on the same page.
- Design the questionnaire so that response choices line up down the page, creating an ordered look.
- If you put labels above the points on a Likert scale, run the labels horizontally rather than vertically; vertical labels are much harder to read.
- For an open-ended question that might receive a comparatively long response, leave ample space for the written answer. If you use lines, leave plenty of space between lines to accommodate variations in handwriting.
- If you include a cover letter (discussed in Chapter 3), an introduction to the questionnaire is unnecessary.
- At the end, include directions for returning the completed questionnaire.

The first page of the PEP questionnaire is included at the end of Chapter 4 as an example of a well-formatted survey instrument.

Question Order

Questions should not be placed haphazardly on the page. In addition to grouping related questions in sections, other considerations should guide question placement.

Begin the questionnaire with easy, interesting questions that apply to every respondent. This type of question will ease a respondent into the task and encourage completion of the questionnaire. Never begin a questionnaire with an open-ended item, and avoid beginning with a set of Likert scales.

Because they can have a negative impact on response rates, demographic questions should appear at the end of the questionnaire. By beginning with demographic, or personal, questions, you risk offending some people, who may then fail to complete and return the questionnaire. The same questions, placed at the end of the questionnaire, are more likely to be answered.

Sensitive Questions

If you have any questions that the respondents may find sensitive (we're not referring here to standard demographic items like income), you should place them in the latter half of the questionnaire, but not immediately preceding the demographics, which are at the very end. Examples include asking employees about company policies, asking patients about the care given by their personal physician, or asking questions about spending habits. Because they are sensitive, these items should not begin a questionnaire. Trust should be established first. However, leaving them to the very end makes it appear—correctly so— that you find them sensitive as well and that you waited to introduce them until no other topics remained.

Skip Patterns

As much as possible, avoid skip patterns (items that don't apply to all respondents). If you must include them, don't have respondents skip more than one page. As much as possible, group questions for the selected respondents together in one skip. And, even though you provide written directions, consider adding graphics to guide the respondent, as shown in Figure 2.1. If you want to go further and draw an arrow directly to the next question, go ahead, as long as it doesn't add clutter.

Figure 2.1   Skip pattern directions

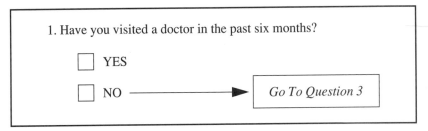

1. Have you visited a doctor in the past six months?

☐ YES

☐ NO ————————➤ *Go To Question 3*

Pretesting

Pretesting is typically the last stage of survey work before data collection begins. Since deadlines for completing the survey are often looming, many investigators are understandably tempted to omit pretesting. Sometimes those paying for the survey don't see the value of pretesting. But questionnaires can't be changed once they have been mailed, and you will have to live with your mistakes.

Our advice here is unequivocal and in line with all good survey practice: you must pretest questionnaires, especially those being used for the first time. Regardless of how much effort has been devoted to developing an effective questionnaire, there *will be* problems that could have been corrected with an adequate pretest.

Pretesting should not be viewed as an activity that begins when the questionnaire is almost finished. Rather, pretesting should be an ongoing process, beginning with colleagues, then branching out to larger audiences and, eventually, the target population.

The goal of a pretest is to find problems in the questionnaire, including poor questions, incomplete directions, and items that are difficult to answer. In conducting pretests, follow these guidelines:

- The number of respondents to include in a formal pretest can't be specified precisely, but we recommend at least 25, preferably 50 to 75 if you plan a statistical analysis of the pretest data. For a formal pretest—one as much like the actual survey as possible—you should include only members of the population you plan to study. And if you intend to statistically analyze the pretest data, you should draw the same type of sample as in the actual study (see Chapter 3 for information on sampling).

- For new studies, perform two pretests. The first aims to correct major problems and will probably look very different from the final questionnaire. It can include more open-ended questions and ask for more comments about the questionnaire itself, such as which questions were unclear or problematic. The second pretest should look as much like the actual survey as possible.

- Consider using focus groups to pretest new questionnaires. Bring together a group of 8 to 12 people and ask them to complete the questionnaire. Follow up with a group discussion about its strengths and weaknesses.

- To determine which response choices to include, use open-ended questions on the pretest to discover the range of possible answers. (Then use a closed form of the same question on the actual survey.)

- To see things from a respondent's perspective, complete the questionnaire yourself.

What to Look For

When analyzing the responses from a pretest, look for these problems or indications of trouble:

- Too little space for open-ended answers.
- Unclear skip patterns.
- Questions with little variance that should probably be dropped.
- Too many skipped questions or *Don't know* responses.
- Too many *Other* responses (so that additional categories must be added).
- Misinterpretation of a question.
- Overlapping response categories.

- Unclear terms.
- Items that incorrectly receive more than one response; multiple-choice questions that don't receive multiple responses.

Remember that some pretesting is better than none, so do as much as you can within the usual constraints of personnel and resources.

3 Sampling and Data Collection

There are many methods for gathering information about the world. For example, you can interview people in their homes, offices, or at a shopping mall, you can send them a questionnaire, or you can call them on the telephone. Regardless of which method you employ, you must also make a decision about how to select the people to contact. Should the respondents be selected to ensure a broad range of characteristics, as is often the case with focus groups? Or should a systematic selection scheme be used?

Regardless of how data are collected, SPSS can be used to analyze the information. However, if you select respondents for a survey haphazardly, you will be unable to generalize the results beyond the survey itself. In other words, a poorly done survey may provide information only about the people in the survey, not about a larger group (which is the fundamental goal of survey research). That is a serious problem.

Samples

Conducting good surveys is both an art and a science, and the process of sampling falls into the latter category. A **sample** is simply a subset of a larger aggregation, typically a **population**, which is defined as the totality of units, or people, that you wish to study (the word "universe" is often used instead of population). The intent is to use the smaller sample to represent the much larger population.

Populations must be carefully defined before sampling can begin. The population for the General Social Survey (GSS), a survey used by many social scientists, is defined as adults aged 18 and over living in households in the United States who can be interviewed in English. Thus, the GSS excludes children and adults living in an institutional setting, such as a college dorm, a nursing home, or a prison.

Probability Sampling

The definition of a sample doesn't mention the concept of probability. That may seem odd, but there are many ways to draw a sample, and only some of them involve the element of probability. A **probability sample** is one in which each element of the population has a known, nonzero chance of being included in the sample. There are several types of probability samples; the most simple is, not surprisingly, the simple random sample (which is discussed on p. 29). Selecting probability samples allows you—with the help of SPSS—to place a level of accuracy, or conversely, error, on the statistics calculated from the sample data. So, if you find that a sample of hospital patients gave the quality of care at a hospital a mean rating of 6.1 (on a seven-point scale), you will be able to further state that the likely rating for all patients at the hospital, including those you didn't contact, is 6.1 plus or minus 0.3 points (in other words, from 5.8 to 6.4). Additionally, using probability samples permits the use of statistical tests to search for group differences, such as those between males and females or those between customers who own different products or use different services.

Nonprobability Sampling

A **nonprobability** sample is one in which a case is chosen in a manner that makes it impossible to estimate or calculate the probability of selection for each element in the population. There are many types of nonprobability samples, including snowball, convenience, or quota sampling. Snowball sampling is often used when population members are hard to identify. It relies upon currently identified sample members to identify other members of the population to be contacted. Convenience sampling relies upon contacting population members who are easily located and willing to participate. Quota sampling divides the population into subgroups (such as male and female, or city, suburban, and rural). Then, based on the proportion of the population in each subgroup, subjects are selected so that the sample matches the population proportions *exactly*, rather than allowing for random variations in the sampling process (see "Stratified Random Sample" on p. 30 for a probability sampling alternative).

There are times when the use of a nonprobability sample is justified; for example, nearly every focus group involves the use of a nonprobability sample, and rightly so. Focus groups are constructed to glean opinions from a wide variety of the target population, especially when being used to pretest a questionnaire. But, given the small size of focus groups, the use of probability sampling methods to choose participants will probably not select participants from the full range of backgrounds and experiences represented in the population. As a consequence, it is more effective to deliberately choose participants for inclusion based on their characteristics to ensure diversity.

The most serious drawback of nonprobability sampling is that it doesn't allow the use of **inferential statistics**, which involve making inferences about the value of a quantity in the population—perhaps the overall level of customer satisfaction—based on statistics calculated from the sample.

The Sampling Process

It should be clear that a probability sample is the best type of sample to use. Given that assumption, how do you actually create a probability sample? The process is summarized in Figure 3.1, which illustrates the key elements of the sampling process.

Figure 3.1   The sampling process

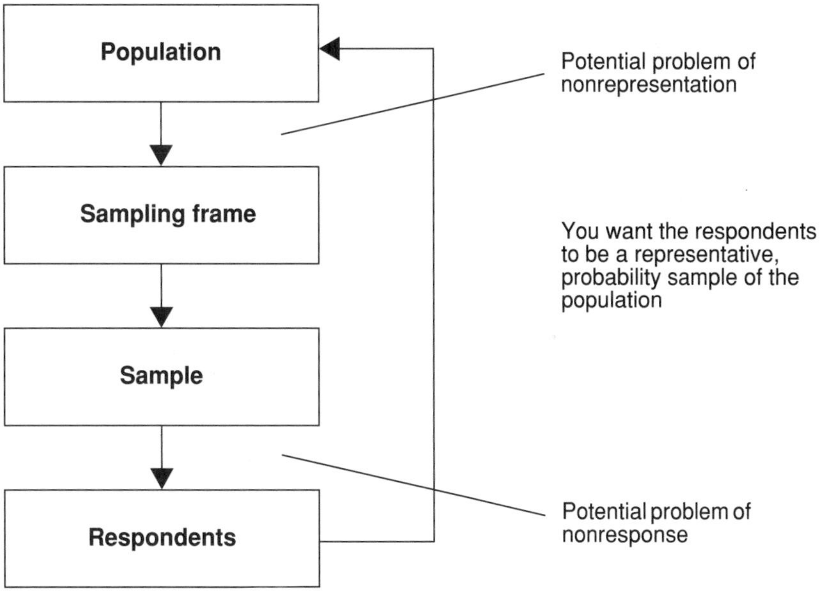

Population

Potential problem of nonrepresentation

Sampling frame

You want the respondents to be a representative, probability sample of the population

Sample

Potential problem of nonresponse

Respondents

Defining the Population

The first step is to define the population of interest. This task might seem trivial, but that's not always the case. Imagine that you are contacting customers of a bank to determine how they feel about its services. If you define the population as all current accounts, you are failing to include the customers who have stopped banking there. As a consequence, you will probably overestimate overall satisfaction with the bank and fail to gather important information about why people chose other financial institutions. To avoid this situation, you should define the population broadly, with little concern about whether all elements of the population can be contacted.

Creating the Sampling Frame

As shown in Figure 3.1, the second stage in sampling is the creation of a sampling frame. The practical limitations of contacting all members of the population are confronted here. A **sampling frame** is a listing of the elements from which you will draw the sample. In the ideal world, the sampling frame will include everyone in the population. Surveys of employees—at least current employees—can create a sampling frame that exactly matches the population of interest, but most of us will have incomplete sampling frames. You should try to ensure that the sampling frame has the following characteristics:

- It is actually created from the target population.
- It is as complete a list as possible of the elements in the population.

As shown in Figure 3.1, problems arise if the sampling frame, when not a complete listing of the population, is a nonrepresentative subset of the population. For example, a list of registered voters used to sample adults in a city would not be a representative sampling frame, since many adults are not registered to vote and they are likely to differ from the former group.

Surveys conducted through the mail are often hampered by incorrect addresses, and every incorrect address causes the sampling frame to be less representative of the population. If a sampling frame cannot be made more complete, it is common to redefine the target population to match the characteristics of the sampling frame (or at least to generalize the results of your survey only to the respondents in the sampling frame, not to the total population). Thus, if you can't list everyone who closed an account at the bank within the past year, the target population can be redefined as only those with current accounts.

Selecting the Sample

Once the sampling frame is available, a sample can be drawn. Notice that we make a distinction between this step, the selection of a sample, and the next stage in the process, where you are concerned with only those who complete and return the questionnaire. We make this distinction because, in terms of survey quality, the lack of correspondence between the respondents and the sample (the total group contacted) is one of the most serious problems in survey research.

There are four basic types of probability samples in survey work, but we will discuss only the three commonly used in mail surveys. All three begin with a list of the population (the sampling frame). To learn about other sample types, see the references on sampling in the bibliography.

Simple Random Sample

A **simple random sample** (SRS) is one in which each element in the sampling frame has a known and equal probability of being selected for the sample. If a hospital admitted 10,000 patients last year and plans to contact 1000 for a survey, an SRS will ensure that each patient has a 1 in 10 (1000/10,000) chance of being in the sample.

An SRS is easy to define but can be difficult to select without careful attention to detail. A series of random numbers, either from a published table or generated by a software program, must be used to select elements from the sampling frame. Following are the key steps in selecting a simple random sample:

1. Decide how many people (elements) should be included in the sample (see "Sample Size" on p. 35).

2. Number the sampling frame list from 1 to N, where N refers to the number for the last element.

3. Generate random numbers by using a table or computer software. If the first random number chosen is 134, the person with that number on the list is selected for the sample.

4. Repeat this process until you have reached the correct sample size.

Systematic Random Sample

The process of selecting an SRS can be quite time consuming. For this reason, samples are often selected with a different, but formally equivalent, technique, called **systematic sampling**. The key to this process is selecting every nth element of a sampling frame rather than using a series of random numbers. Following are the steps in selecting a systematic random sample:

1. As with an SRS, decide how many elements should be in the sample.

2. Calculate the sampling fraction, defined as $1/n$. For example, the hospital that plans to survey its patients has a list of 10,000 but needs to contact only 1000. They must sample 1/10 of the population, or 1 in every 10 patients. $1/n$ is the sampling fraction, where $n=10$.

3. Use a random number table (just one time) to pick a number within the sampling interval from 1 to n (for the hospital, the interval runs from 1 to 10). Let's call this random number S_n.

4. Pick the S_nth element in the sampling frame as the first person in the sample. If the researcher for the hospital had chosen 5 as the random starting point, he or she would pick the fifth patient on the list.

5. Now add n to S_n ($5 + 10 = 15$ for the hospital), and choose that element next. Then add n to this number and choose that element, and so on, until you reach the end of the list (the hospital will choose the 5th, 15th, 25th, 35th, etc., patients on its sampling frame).

This process is straightforward and can be automated if your sampling frame is in a computer database. However, two problems can arise with systematic samples:

- If you miscalculate the sampling interval, you may have too few or too many elements in the sample. This can be easily corrected in various ways (for example, you can drop elements randomly if too many are chosen). Clearly, having a good original estimate of the number of elements in the sampling frame makes the process of systematic sampling more efficient.

- If the sampling frame has a cycle embedded in it, it is possible that the sampling interval chosen may cause you to draw a nonrepresentative sample. Lists structured by zip code, date, or alphabetized by name are normally not a problem. But imagine a list of customers for the Personal Electronic Products (PEP) company that is sorted so that the first customer owns a fax machine, the second, a personal copier, the third, a fax machine, and so on, alternating until the end of the sampling frame. If you choose a sampling interval of 2 and begin with the second customer, you will choose only customers who own personal copiers. It is usually easy to discover cyclic order on a list and correct it, either by reordering the sampling frame or choosing a different sampling interval.

Stratified Random Sample

Stratified sampling requires more than making a list of elements (and estimating the number of elements on the list). It also involves purposely ordering that list by subgroups (or strata) and then sampling randomly within those subgroups. This method of sampling is used for two reasons:

- It can reduce the errors in the statistical estimates calculated from the sample.

- It allows you to create a sample that is exactly representative of the various subgroups in the population that you find to be of special interest. For example, the hospital may decide to stratify by sex, age, or type of treatment (or all of these simultaneously) because these are all important characteristics of patients.

There are two types of stratified samples:

- A **proportionate stratified sample** selects the number of elements from each stratum so that the stratum sample size is proportional to the stratum population size. Let's say the hospital stratifies by age, dividing the population into those who are age 50 or above and those who are under 50. If there are twice as many people aged 50 or above admitted to the hospital as those under 50, a proportionate stratified sample will include twice as many people aged 50 or above.

If you create a disproportionate sample, you will need to weight the data to present summaries for the sample as a whole. You can do this with the SPSS WEIGHT command.

- A **disproportionate stratified sample** selects the number of elements from each stratum so that the stratum sample size is not proportional to the stratum population size. The most common reason for selecting this type of sample is when you want to study a relatively rare but important subpopulation, such as younger patients suffering from heart disease. Proportionate stratification may result in too few elements being selected so that little, if any, statistical analysis can be done. Consequently, even if these patients represent only 1% of the population, you might decide to make them 10% of the final sample.

Selecting a stratified sample is not that different from selecting a simple or systematic random sample, once you have divided the sampling frame into strata. You must estimate the number of elements in each stratum and use the SRS methods outlined above within each stratum to select the sample. Even when you don't plan to do separate analyses by stratum, drawing a proportionate stratified sample is a good idea—when there are important subgroups in the population—because it ensures a sample that is perfectly representative of the population on the characteristics used to create the strata.

If the population list is stored electronically, an easy way to draw a proportionate stratified sample is to sort the list based on the variables used to define the stratum, and then use the techniques described for systematic random sampling to select the sample. This procedure automatically selects a proportionate number from each stratum without calculations (except, of course, for the overall sample size calculation). For example, if two variables, gender and income, are used to define the stratum, with the income stratum defined separately for males and females, first sort the file by gender and then by income within each gender category. Unfortunately, no such simple technique exists to select a disproportionate stratified sample.

Contacting the Respondents

After you have chosen a sample, the next step is to contact those specific elements (people) from the sampling frame and provide them with the questionnaire. Although not difficult, this task can be time consuming because it includes many details, such as stuffing envelopes, putting on postage and labels, etc. And you should be aware that there can be potential problems when you move your attention from selecting the sample to the **respondents**, the group who actually answers the questionnaire.

The process up to this point has basically been under your control. You may often have a complete list of the population, and if not, at least a good idea of the limitations of the sampling frame. And if you're careful, you can correctly define and select one of the three types of samples discussed above. But after the questionnaires are in the mail, you are dependent on the U.S. Postal Service and the whims and vagaries of the potential respondents. If, for whatever reason, those who choose to complete the questionnaire differ in some important attributes from those who do not, the respondents will not be representative of the sample. And since the sample is representative of the sampling frame, which is representative of the population, the respondents will then not be representative of the population. This is potentially a very serious problem, and it is always a concern when response rates fall much below 70% to 80% (that is, when the number of respondents is less than that fraction of the sample size).

If, on the other hand, all goes well, at the end of the survey process you will have collected data from a group of respondents that is a representative, probability sample of the total population. You will know what elements in the population may not be represented because of deficiencies in the sampling frame, and you will be able to use SPSS to calculate the amount of sampling error in the data.

Sampling Error

By definition, when you have collected a sample from a population, you have less than complete information about the population. This, in turn, means that there is a chance that the sample statistics you calculate—for example, the mean of a variable, a frequency distribution, etc.—may not be equal to those same values in the population. In fact, you would have to be extraordinarily fortunate for the sample statistic to be *exactly* equal to the population value (a population value is called a **parameter**).

The error in the sample estimate is not an intrinsic impediment to analysis. For probability samples, sampling theory allows you to calculate the expected amount of error given a particular sample size, sampling method, and the specific statistic of interest. In general terms, the sampling error for any statistic can be defined as

$$\text{standard error} \;=\; \sqrt{\dfrac{\text{variance}}{N}} \qquad\qquad \textbf{Equation 3.1}$$

where N refers to the number of respondents. As the sample size increases, the standard error of a statistic decreases; as the variance, or dispersion, of a statistic increases, so does its sampling error.

Calculations in SPSS assume both simple random sampling and a sample size much smaller than the population size. If one or both of these assumptions is violated, you may have to use another formula to calculate sampling error (see the bibliography). In practice, it is usually reasonable to use the statistical tests calculated by SPSS without adjustment for the samples discussed here because they result in a more conservative test of your hypothesis.

In Equation 3.1, a term representing the population size does not appear. Unless your sample size is greater than about 10% of the population size, you can ignore the population size when calculating the sampling error. Note also that because of the square root, increasing the sample size by a factor of 4 only decreases the error by a factor of 2. Figure 3.2 shows the relationship between sample size and sampling error for a dichotomous variable, in this case, a variable measuring whether or not someone is likely to buy another product from the PEP company.

Figure 3.2   Relationship of sample size to sampling error

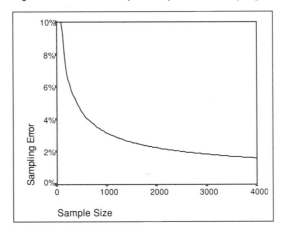

Sampling error decreases rapidly as the sample size increases from a few hundred to about 1000 respondents. After that point, the reduction in error comes more slowly. This relationship between sample size and error is one of the principal reasons why national surveys conducted by Roper, Gallup, and news organizations have sample sizes of approximately 1000 to 1500. For estimating proportions—such as the percentage of people who would vote for a political candidate—a sample of that size has an error of approximately $\pm 3\%$. The trade-off in increased cost versus reduction in error for larger samples is such that there is rarely any reason to select larger samples (but see "Calculating the Sample Size" on p. 36).

The formula for the standard error of a proportion is simple and easy to apply:

$$\text{standard error} = \sqrt{\frac{(p) \times (1-p)}{N}} \qquad \text{Equation 3.2}$$

Here, p represents the proportion of interest (those who say they will buy again from PEP), $1-p$ represents the proportion giving the opposite response, and N is the total number of responses. The standard error statistic is greatest when p and $1-p$ are equal, which occurs when each is 0.50, or 50%, of the sample.

Nonsampling Error

Before discussing how to determine sample size, we will briefly review other sources of error in surveys. When you read an article in *Time* or *Newsweek* reporting on the results of a national poll, the error in the estimates is always listed, derived, generally speaking, from Equation 3.2. However, experienced survey researchers know that errors due to other sources are typically greater than the error due to sampling alone! Following are some other types of errors:

- Measurement errors, caused by poorly written questions, poorly designed questionnaires, respondent errors in completing questionnaires, and so on.

- Nonresponse errors, caused because the respondents are not a representative subset of the population.

- Data coding errors, caused by errors in coding and entering the data.

Of these error sources, the first two are typically more severe. In mail surveys, nonresponse error is often the most serious problem.

There are two critical characteristics of these nonsampling errors. First, as mentioned above, their sum is often greater than the sampling error. Second, and more insidious, these errors are often impossible to estimate for any one survey, especially measurement and nonresponse errors. Consequently, using Equation 3.1 and Equation 3.2 to estimate the error in a statistic often provides a false sense of security.

Experienced survey researchers take this fact into account by being more cautious in discussing survey results than the sampling error alone would indicate, and you should do the same. Ideally, the other sources of error would balance themselves out so that errors in one direction negate errors in the other direction, but you cannot assume that this is the case.

Sample Size

You can use a variety of methods to calculate the sample size necessary for your study (remember, sample size refers to the number of *respondents* you require). Some methods are more complex than others, but all are based on the fundamental concept of how much error you are willing to tolerate in a statistical estimate.

Confidence Intervals

When you estimate a characteristic of the population from a survey, such as the number of people willing to recommend PEP products, your goal is to be able to make a statement like *We estimate that 45% of our current customers will recommend PEP products, plus or minus 4%, at the 95% confidence level.*

The standard error discussed above is not the exact sampling error. Instead, the standard error is transformed into the sample (statistic) error by using the confidence interval. The theory of probability sampling allows you to place a confidence interval around any statistic by using the definitional formula shown in Equation 3.3:

Figure 3.2 was created by using the formula shown in Equation 3.3.

$$\text{confidence interval} = \text{statistic} \pm (Z \times \text{standard error}) \qquad \textbf{Equation 3.3}$$

The confidence interval is the estimate of sampling error. Notice that the standard error is multiplied by a scaling factor, called Z, which is the z score associated with the level of confidence you want (a sufficiently large sample that allows the use of the normal curve is assumed here). The 95% confidence level is associated with a z score of 1.96, so you multiply the standard error by 1.96 to get the confidence interval around the statistic. You will learn more about this concept in later chapters on data analysis.

Why is Equation 3.3 important? Recall that the formula for the standard error includes N, the number of respondents in your study (see Equation 3.1). Therefore, by plugging Equation 3.1 into Equation 3.3 and solving for N, you can derive a formula for sample size.

Calculating the Sample Size

It is a common misconception that the sample size is somehow determined by the size of the population, but for most surveys this is not true (remember that the population size did not appear in the calculation of the standard error). That is why samples of 1500 are considered adequate to describe characteristics of large populations.

The classic approach to calculate sample size is to choose a margin of acceptable error and then use that value in a calculation. You can do this with either statistical tables, software, or the formula shown in Equation 3.4 for categorical data:

$$N = \frac{Z^2}{4 \times (\text{acceptable error})^2}$$

Equation 3.4

Here, Z again refers to the z score associated with the level of confidence you want. At the 95% confidence level, the equation becomes

$$N = \frac{1}{(\text{acceptable error})^2}$$

Equation 3.5

where the z value of 1.96 has been rounded to 2 (which makes the calculation more conservative). For example, let's assume you find an error of $\pm 5\%$ acceptable when estimating the proportion of a population that would buy a product or use a service again. Then the required sample size is $1/(0.05)^2$, or 400 people.

Nevertheless, this approach is not as straightforward or useful as it might seem. In most situations, you are interested in a number of variables, and it is impossible to simultaneously find *one* sample size suitable for each margin of error (which will differ from one variable to another). And setting an acceptable margin of error may not be an easy task without experience from previous surveys and other information.

The upshot of these considerations is that you do not have to determine the sample size via a precise calculation; in most cases, it will be sufficient to keep in mind the following guidelines:

- Base the sample size first on a minimally adequate sample size for the important subgroups in the population. You should strive to include at least 50 respondents, preferably 100, in each important subgroup. A hospital surveying patients could plan to include at least 50 patients who had cancer, 50 with heart disease, 50 women who gave birth, and so on, if each of these was an important subgroup worth studying separately and comparing to the other groups or total group of respondents. Add together the subsamples to get the minimally adequate total sample size.

- Given the relationship shown in Figure 3.2, there is rarely a good reason for sample sizes above 1500 or so, as long as an adequate subgroup sample size has been taken into account.

- The resources available must be allocated wisely, and there may simply not be enough money to sample beyond a fixed size determined by the estimated costs of mailing, data cleaning and coding, etc. If money is tight, draw a smaller initial sample and try to obtain higher response rates, instead of the reverse.

- If it is possible to specify a minimum acceptable level of error, you can use an equation or the tables in various books (for example, Fowler, 1993) to determine the minimum acceptable subgroup sample sizes that might be above the level of 50 to 100 recommended above (they are unlikely to be much lower than these numbers).

- If resources are available and a deadline is not approaching, on the average, larger sample sizes are preferable to smaller sizes. And, of course, if your sampling process ends up with 5000 returned questionnaires, that is just fine. You may not need that number of responses, given the other considerations above, but the larger the sample, the lower the sampling error.

In Figure 3.1, we differentiated between the sample and the respondents. The calculation of the sample size is concerned with the number of respondents required. To determine the number to select for the sample drawn from the sampling frame, you must estimate the nonresponse rate. The actual sample size to be drawn is

$$\text{sample size} \ = \ \frac{\text{number of respondents}}{\text{response rate}} \qquad \text{Equation 3.6}$$

So, if the PEP company decides that they need 700 respondents, and the expected response rate from their customers is 50%, then 700/0.50, or 1400, customers must be drawn from the sampling frame.

A risk in the data analysis phase is that the larger the sample, the more likely you are to find a difference between subgroups to be statistically significant. Small, trivial differences will be statistically distinct, leading you to make decisions based on statistical rather than substantive criteria.

Data Collection

The most hectic moments in the survey process occur during the mailing of materials. You should monitor the work very closely so that letters are matched with envelopes for the same respondent, all pieces get placed in each envelope, and so on. It is usually not too difficult to create labels, stuff materials into envelopes, put postage on them, and wait for the returned questionnaires. The key to quality in data collection, after a first-rate questionnaire has been developed, is to convince the respondents to complete and return the questionnaire in a timely manner.

Nonresponse

Many people who understand something about sampling error—but not perhaps response rates—believe that if they send out enough questionnaires and get back 500 to 1000, their survey has been successful. With this many respondents, they reason, the sampling error will be reasonably small. But what if the response rate is low, say 15%? Does the low response rate cause an increase in error?

Those who argue that a low response rate doesn't preclude reporting the results of a survey base their argument on both faith and technical considerations. It is true that nonresponse, *by itself*, is not a cause for concern. High enough levels of nonresponse, of course, mean that more people must be contacted initially to ensure enough returned questionnaires for statistical analysis. But to the extent that the nonrespondents do not differ from the respondents with regard to the critical variables, the statistical estimates from the survey will be close to those in the population.

Unfortunately, it is typically true that as nonresponse increases, the likelihood that the nonrespondents differ from the respondents in an important way becomes more and more certain. In satisfaction studies of all types, if vigorous efforts are not used to increase response rates, the most likely responders are often thought to be those with complaints and problems who have lower overall satisfaction. Low response rates would therefore skew a survey's measure of overall satisfaction, lowering it below the total population value. This is just one example of why you must strive to increase the response rate.

Acceptable Response Rates

There are no agreed-upon standards for what constitutes a good response rate. National surveys conducted over the telephone or by personal interview expect to achieve rates above 80%. Mail surveys have lower response rates, but it is possible, with a lot of effort, to get rates near that level. Keep in mind the following three points when you assess the response rate:

- If you achieve response rates of 80% or above, you won't have to worry about nonresponse.

- If response rates fall below 50%, you have a potential problem, since there are more nonrespondents than respondents. When the nonrespondents have different opinions or characteristics, the survey results will be biased.

- If response rates fall low enough, you should be cautious in presenting or acting upon the survey results.

Try to compare the respondents to the nonrespondents whenever possible. Often, as long as the survey is confidential, you may already have some information about the people selected in the sample (customer records might be helpful here). See if the nonrespondents differ in gender, age, place of residence, and other characteristics. For important surveys, it is common to contact some of the nonrespondents after the deadline (either by phone or with a short mailed questionnaire) to gather some comparison data. The more similar the nonrespondents are to the respondents, the more confident you can be that a low response rate doesn't bias the survey results.

Getting Higher Response Rates

In real estate, the key is "location, location, location." In survey research, the key is "contact, contact, contact." Sending out one mailing with no follow-up is likely to obtain a response rate of no more than 20%. At least three contacts with the sample, each slightly different in tone and content, are necessary to ensure a high return.

Cover Letters

Chapter 2 discussed how the questionnaire should be formatted to reduce errors and increase response. Include a cover letter with all but the most brief questionnaires, or, if you prefer, put the information listed below on the cover of the questionnaire. A cover letter should have the following characteristics:

- Keep it brief (no more than one page) and concise, write in an interesting style designed to draw the interest of the reader, and thank the respondent for participating.
- Personalize it by using the respondent's name in the salutation (unless there is a concern, as for employee surveys).
- Mention the purpose of the study, how and why the respondent was chosen, and the sponsoring organization (if appropriate).
- Explain why the study is important to your organization and the respondent.
- Explain that the study is confidential/anonymous and how the information will be used.
- Provide a soft deadline (such as *Please try to respond within a week or two*) rather than a fixed date.
- Explain how to return the questionnaire and who to contact if the respondent has any questions.

A sample cover letter using these principles from one of PEP's surveys is shown in Figure 3.3.

Figure 3.3   Sample cover letter

PEP
100 Industrial Drive
Chicago, IL 60607
Tel: 312-555-1212
Fax: 312-555-3434

Dear Mr. Smith:

We'd like to get your views on how to improve PEP products!

We're contacting current owners of PEP fax machines and personal copiers to learn more about how you use and like our products. PEP is currently engaged in several long-term studies designed to understand how our products help people get things done and, just as important, how we can improve our products to help you and others. Please share your views with us about these topics so that we can improve PEP products for you and other customers.

Your name was randomly selected from our existing database for inclusion in this study. Please be assured that all information you provide will be treated in a confidential manner, and that no names will be attached to individual responses.

We've enclosed a postage-paid envelope for your convenience in returning the questionnaire. If you have any questions about the survey, please contact me directly.

Thanks for your participation in this study.

Sincerely,

John Doe

John Doe
President, PEP

Mailing Details

Questionnaires should always be sent by first-class mail, although research shows only a slight advantage compared to metered mail. The return postage should always be paid by your organization, and putting a stamp on the return envelope will increase response rates slightly compared to using a business permit. If funds are available, the questionnaire can be sent via express mail, certified mail, or a carrier other than the U.S. Postal Service, but this is an expensive way to increase response rates.

Mailing Sequence

Follow these steps to ensure a successful survey:

1. Send the first mailing with a cover letter, questionnaire, and return envelope.

2. After about 10 days and no more than 14 days, send the entire sample a reminder postcard, emphasizing the importance of the study and thanking those who have already responded and those who will respond.

Step 3 in the mailing sequence requires careful timing and a quick, accurate recording of who has responded. The chance for error is greatest here, so review the procedure you'll be using closely.

3. About two weeks later, mail all nonrespondents another questionnaire plus a new, shorter cover letter, with another return envelope.

For even higher response rates, try one or both of these techniques:

- Send a notification postcard before the first mailing, telling the respondent that a survey is coming.

- Call all those who didn't respond to the third mailing.

You will have received over 90% of all questionnaires approximately eight weeks after the first mailing, so plan accordingly. As explained in Chapter 4, data coding can begin before then, particularly if the survey results must be produced quickly.

Anonymity

If your survey is to be anonymous—so that even you don't know who completed a particular questionnaire—how do you know to whom to mail a second questionnaire? A standard technique is to include a separate postcard in the first mailing with an ID number (the questionnaire won't have an ID). The postcard is sent back separately from the questionnaire, and on it is printed a statement like *I have returned my questionnaire. Thanks for not sending me any more reminders.*

Incentives

Providing a small monetary or other inducement is an effective additional means to increase the response rate. If the funds are available, incentives will increase response rates by as much as 20%. The trick is to offer the inducement in a way that increases the response rate but doesn't affect the survey responses.

Monetary Incentives

Always send the money along with the questionnaire, rather than making the incentive dependent upon a completed questionnaire. Modest sums of money are adequate—an amount between one and five dollars should suffice for surveys of the general public. Surveys of lawyers, doctors, and other professionals might need to include a larger amount. Send cash rather than a check whenever possible.

Offering a chance in a drawing or lottery for a large prize, such as a trip to Hawaii or a color television, is a reasonable alternative. In this case, the prize is available only to those who return the questionnaire. This often costs less than sending money to everyone, but it will probably produce a lesser improvement in the response rate.

Nonmonetary Incentives

Some surveys include key chains, buttons, golf balls, coupons, or other novelties. Research indicates that this approach is not nearly as effective as sending cash. However, for a special population and a desirable gift, it might be very effective. As with the cash incentive, the gift should not be contingent upon return of the questionnaire.

The area of incentives is a chance to be creative and experiment. If your organization can offer a service to the respondent that he or she will value, such as a report of the results or a donation to a designated charity for every returned questionnaire, give it a try.

4 Defining and Entering Data

The questionnaires have now been returned and logged in. The task now is to construct an SPSS data set that is as error-free as possible from all that paper. As with the procedures for mailing questionnaires and reducing nonresponse, coding and cleaning data require mostly hard work and attention to detail. So, if you and your colleagues put in the effort, success at these tasks is highly probable.

Coding of data entails preparing a set of rules or procedures that transforms the survey responses into codes for entry into a software program. The amount of coding to be accomplished will vary quite a bit from one survey to the next. **Data entry** is the physical act of typing data into a program (when done in the SPSS Data Editor, an SPSS data file is created). Data entry also includes labeling the data so that, say, you know that a code of 1 refers to a response of *Yes* for a specific question.

As discussed in previous chapters, steps can be taken early in the survey process to make the tasks of coding and entering data more straightforward:

- Response choices are numbered.
- Each returned questionnaire has a unique identification number.

If each respondent answers all items (so that there is no missing data), all questions are close-ended in format, and no problems exist with the mismarking of a response, then data entry can begin soon after the questionnaires are received. In most cases, though, there are likely to be some open-ended items that demand special attention, and there will surely be missing data, plus respondent errors (such as answering a question that didn't apply). Data entry can't proceed until these issues or problems are resolved.

Most software that can be used for data entry is quite flexible, so the type of software program you will be using—whether SPSS or some other choice—should not enter into the coding decisions you make. Instead, response choices should be coded to minimize data entry error and to facilitate later data analysis. An important rule to follow in all coding is to use numeric codes as much as possible. SPSS can read and manipulate both numeric and alphanumeric data, but it is far easier for you to label, analyze, and report on data stored in numeric format.

Coding the Data

Regardless of who will be coding and entering the data, it is necessary to prepare a comprehensive set of written guidelines. Include instructions about what to do with mismarked responses (for example, assign the items a "missing" code), open-ended responses (for example, code as 7 any response that uses the word "problem"), and so on.

Develop the instructions as you review the questionnaires. Although you will save time by beginning the job of coding before all questionnaires have been received, be careful to review a substantial number of the questionnaires before you establish a coding scheme.

Identification Number

Your questionnaires may contain ID numbers if the survey was confidential, or contain no ID number if the survey was anonymous. In either instance, an ID number must be entered into the data file to link the questionnaires and the data file records (or *cases*, as SPSS labels each row in the Data Editor). If there is no identification number on the questionnaire, number each consecutively as it is received, then use that number for data entry. In some cases, although there is an ID number available, you may not wish to use it in the data file because the number would allow respondents to be matched to an existing database. As an alternative, number the questionnaires consecutively as each is received and use that number as the ID. (You can go one step further and remove the original ID from the questionnaire for maximum security.)

Reviewing the Questionnaires

Examine the returned questionnaires, looking especially for the following problems:

- Any indications that the respondent did not carefully complete the questionnaire. This can include written comments in the margins, very sloppy marking, a response set (selecting a code of 5 for every Likert scale item), or a large number of missing responses. If problems are great enough, you might decide to delete this person from the study.

- Errors that can be fixed, such as incorrectly answered skip-and-fill responses (assign the *Not applicable* code instead), multiple responses to questions that request only one choice (you may decide to pick the first response selected, pick randomly from the choices, or code the question as missing data), items left blank that can be coded (for example, if the survey is confidential so that respondents can be identified, there may be information from an existing database that can be added).

- Anything unclear or out of the ordinary that should be addressed. For example, if the respondent has marked *Highly dissatisfied* for the individual attributes question but has left the overall satisfaction question blank, code that item as *Highly dissatisfied* (code of 1) as well.

Coding Guidelines

Before you begin to create specific codes for each question, you must understand the logical link between your questions and the data you will create in SPSS.

Each response to a question becomes a **variable** in SPSS and occupies one column in the Data Editor. In most instances, questions request only a single response, so each question is equivalent to an SPSS variable. Thus, in the PEP questionnaire at the end of this chapter, the first question asks which product a respondent owns. Only one answer is allowed per respondent, so that question will become an SPSS variable (which we will call *product*). The response to this question, either a 1 or 2, will be entered in the field or column for *product*.

The exception to this is multiple response items, which by design can have more than one response to a single question. In that instance, each response may become a separate variable (see "Coding Multiple Response Items" on p. 50).

As you work through the questionnaire and develop coding schemes for items, think about these issues and make sure you know which questions have only one response and which are, instead, multiple response items. These rules apply whether you plan to enter the data into SPSS directly or into a spreadsheet or database program first.

Creating Consistent Codes

One of the best methods to ensure accurate data entry and more efficient data analysis is to use a coding scheme that gives the same numeric values to similar responses. For questions with response choices of only *Yes* and *No*, code the former with the same code on each question. Typical codes are 0 and 1, or 1 and 2, for the two responses. It doesn't really matter what the numbers are as long as you are consistent.

The same advice holds for Likert scales; that is, code the response indicating the highest level of satisfaction, for example, with the highest value on the scale, and code the lowest level with the lowest value. This coding scheme can be adopted when the questionnaire is created, as discussed in Chapter 2. However, what if you've reversed response scales, as was also suggested in that chapter? In that case, enter the data as coded on the questionnaire, and then recode the item in SPSS to match the other Likert-type items. See Chapter 5 for information on the Recode procedure.

Coding Missing Data

Missing data are common in surveys, for many legitimate reasons. There are generally three ways for data to become missing, and SPSS has provided for these by allowing the definition of three missing codes for each variable.

Not Applicable. When a respondent skips a question because it does not apply, a corresponding code should be entered. For example, question 6 asks about whether a product was repaired satisfactorily (variable *repair),* which is answered only by those customers whose product failed to operate correctly. Those who correctly skipped this question will have no response, but it is best to assign them a numeric code that indicates that fact.

If "No response" and a response of "Don't know" are to be treated separately, be sure to include an explicit response choice for "Don't know."

Don't Know. It is perfectly acceptable for a respondent to indicate that he or she doesn't know the answer to a question. For factual items (*Did you speak with a sale representative in the past three months?*) this type of response is normally caused by a failure of memory. For opinion or attitude items (*What is your overall satisfaction with the product?*), it is typically the result of conflicting attitudes, lack of familiarity with the subject of the question, or lack of interest in the topic.

No Response. Some respondents leave questions blank, which is often not equivalent to choosing *Don't know.* A respondent may have forgotten to answer an item (this occurs fairly often in self-administered surveys), may refuse to answer a question (items about income suffer this fate), or may not have found a choice that corresponds to the preferred response. And, to complicate things, if a question doesn't include an explicit *Don't know* option, it is possible that leaving the question blank is the same as choosing *Don't know.*

As far as SPSS is concerned, missing data are not left blank but are normally assigned a code for data entry. Each of the possible types of missing data should be given a code, and the code should be consistent across questions. Thus, for all scale items, you might assign a code of 8 for *No response,* a code of 9 for *Don't know*, and a code of 0 for *Not applicable*. The exact codes are not important as long as you don't choose a code used for a valid response for that question. For questions with two digits for input (age is an example), codes of 98, 99, or 0 could be assigned as missing values.

These data are called **user-missing** because the user tells SPSS what to define as missing. These responses will not be used by SPSS for data analysis unless you instruct otherwise.

Nevertheless, there are times when you might want to leave a field blank, often to signify the *No response* choice, or for ease of data entry. If you do, SPSS automatically assigns a special missing value, called **system-missing**, which is indicated with a period (.). As with user-missing values, SPSS does not use system-missing values for analysis unless you instruct otherwise. You can, therefore, actually have four different types of missing values for each variable in SPSS, although you cannot assign a label to the system-missing value to identify it further.

Coding Open-Ended Items

Many surveys include items asking the respondent to provide a nonstructured response (*What else do you like about the product?* or *How should we modify our repair service to improve its effectiveness?*). There are generally two methods to code these responses.

Coding Responses Exactly

Rather than losing any detail, it is tempting to enter an open-ended response exactly as written. SPSS can be used for this purpose, and alphanumeric variables can be created, up to 255 characters in length. This option should normally be avoided, primarily because it provides too much information and makes it impossible to easily summarize the responses to a question. Also, SPSS provides fewer facilities for reporting on these **long string variables**.

Creating Numeric Codes for Similar Responses

The benefit of open-ended questions is that they give the respondent freedom to provide a complete and unstructured response; however, that doesn't imply that a framework shouldn't be imposed on the answers. For example, if asked how our repair service can be improved, two separate comments of *Improve speed of initial response* and *Initial response was slow* might well be judged to be essentially identical. If so, they can be given the same numeric code and treated as identical for analysis. Remember that SPSS functions best with numeric data.

The challenge is to create a set of codes that are comprehensive, can be applied consistently, and that create a reasonable number of distinct categories. Following are some guidelines:

- Be sure you understand how a question will be used in the analysis and which differences between responses are of practical importance. In other words, specify the goal of any coding scheme beforehand so that it can guide the coding process.

To measure the agreement between two raters, use the Crosstabs procedure with the kappa statistic.

- When developing a coding scheme, code the first 25 returned questionnaires; then apply the scheme to another 25 to see how well it performs.

- Develop a coding scheme with a moderate number of categories—no more than 10–20. More than this defeats the purpose of creating codes for grouping answers.

- When in doubt, create more, rather than fewer, codes, since codes you later see as similar can be combined later, either by hand or in SPSS.

- To check the reliability of the coding, have at least two people code the same questionnaires, using the coding instructions you've developed. Better than 90% agreement is excellent, and anything over 70% is usually acceptable.

- If people list several things in a response, coding only the first two or three is sufficient for most purposes.

Coding Multiple Response Items

It is very likely that you will write questions that request more than one response from each person. For example, if you ask a respondent to check each feature of a product that he or she uses or ask which magazines they read regularly, most respondents will supply several answers to this one question.

Multiple response items can be coded in two formats, both of which can be used by SPSS to produce equivalent output. The format you use doesn't depend on how the questionnaire is formatted, although some formats lend themselves more readily to one coding scheme or the other. Instead, the choice between coding formats is based on other criteria, such as reduction in the necessary number of keystrokes for data entry.

Multiple Dichotomy Coding

If a variable (column in the Data Editor window) is created for each of the response choices, then **multiple dichotomy** coding is being used. When a response choice is selected (reads *Time* magazine), a variable corresponding to that choice is coded with a 1. If not selected, a code of 0 is assigned. Clearly, if there are many possible choices, multiple dichotomy coding requires the addition of many variables to the data file, which can be a disadvantage. Data entry for this type of coding is often very accurate, however, since you need note only whether a response is checked or not (often from a list of items on the questionnaire itself). Multiple dichotomy coding is also useful when the maximum number of responses can't be estimated in advance.

Multiple Response Coding

When only enough variables are created to correspond to the maximum number of possible responses, and codes are used to specify a particular choice, **multiple response** coding is being used (note that this phrase is also used to describe this general type of question). In our example of magazine reading habits, if no one respondent reads more than 10 magazines regularly, then only 10 variables need be created. Each possible response is given a code (for *Time* magazine, it might be 17). Then, when anyone lists *Time* magazine, one of the ten variables (it really doesn't matter which one) is given the prespecified code for that publication—17. In multiple response coding, most respondents will not list the maximum number of possible choices; in that event, the extra variables can either be left blank or given a special code—say, 0—which will later be defined as missing. If it is possible to estimate the maximum number of responses to a question, multiple response coding is often a better choice.

It must be emphasized that no one scheme is better than another for purposes of analysis and reporting. Both will get the job done and both can be used by SPSS. For ease of data entry, if multiple response coding is to be used with response choices supplied on the questionnaire, we recommend including the assigned code with the choice. For the magazine question, a portion of the response choices might be formatted as follows (where the respondent has chosen *Time* magazine):

(17) Time

18 Newsweek

19 Scientific American

and so on. This makes it easy to enter the correct value and avoids the potential for error in referring to a list.

We consider below how to label multiple dichotomy and multiple response variables. Without appropriate labels, you won't be able to interpret the reports that SPSS produces with multiple response data.

Data Entry

Once coding has been accomplished, the next step is data entry. Although we are using SPSS for data entry, we will also briefly consider other options.

Before personal computers were widely available, data entry was accomplished on mainframe computers or keypunch machines. Now, data entry has become streamlined, and options for creating data files have increased. In addition to using the Data Editor to create SPSS data files, you can create three other types of data files, all of which can be read by SPSS.

ASCII Files

Data that have been typed into a text editor, such as Notepad, or into a word processing program, such as Microsoft Word, and then saved as a text file are in ASCII format. SPSS can read these files with the Read ASCII Data or Open options from the File menu. Text files can be created in three varieties:

- **Fixed format.** Information for each variable is in a fixed number of columns for each respondent.
- **Tab-delimited.** Data values are separated by tabs.
- **Freefield.** Data values are separated by at least one space.

We recommend against using ASCII files because the creation of such files, especially in fixed and freefield formats, is prone to error. Other methods are more efficient and give you more options for transferring data to other software programs.

Spreadsheet Files

See the SPSS Base User's Guide for information on reading spreadsheet and database files into SPSS.

It's very likely that you've used a spreadsheet program such as Lotus 1-2-3 or Microsoft Excel in your work. These programs can readily be used for data entry, and their general format—a rectangular set of rows and columns—matches that of the SPSS Data Editor.

Spreadsheet programs are convenient to use for data entry because each column can, and should, be given an identifying name, which will be retained by SPSS, and a simple keystroke moves you from column to column as data are entered. SPSS can read Lotus 1-2-3, Excel, and SYLK spreadsheet formats directly. If you are using another spreadsheet program, such as Quattro Pro, it is very likely that the data can be saved in one or more of these three formats.

When a spreadsheet file is read by SPSS, the only information you may have to supply, besides the filename and file type, is illustrated in Figure 4.1 in the Opening File Options dialog box.

Figure 4.1   Opening File Options dialog box for spreadsheet files

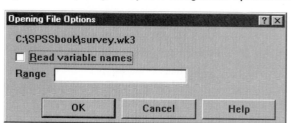

If you have labeled the columns in the spreadsheet program, select Read Variable names. (When you label the columns, try to use names of eight characters or less to match the SPSS variable name specification.) If you don't want SPSS to read the full range of rows and columns in the spreadsheet, you can supply a range specification (specific to each spreadsheet type) in the Range text box.

Database Files

Database programs have a common format that is, in some respects, even more convenient for data entry than a spreadsheet program. The chief advantage is that the user can create data entry screens that are similar in appearance to the actual questionnaire, which reduces errors in data entry. Moreover, after a field's value has been entered, the cursor can be programmed to move automatically to the next field.

Database files are logically very similar to SPSS data files. SPSS automatically translates the field names (again, limit the names to eight or fewer characters) into SPSS variable names and reads the whole file. Thus, after the data have been entered into the database, you need only specify the filename and file type for SPSS to be able to read the data file. SPSS reads dBASE files directly; if you are using another program, such as Microsoft Access, you can easily create a dBASE-format file in Access and then read the data into SPSS.

Using the SPSS Data Editor

The Data Editor in SPSS provides a convenient method for creating data files that is similar, for purposes of data entry, to spreadsheet programs. The important difference is that typing the data into the Data Editor automatically creates an SPSS data file, which simplifies the process of preparing the data for analysis.

The Data Editor also provides facilities for labeling variables (the questions) and individual data values, defining missing values, and modifying display formats. Before you enter any data, you should define the variables in SPSS.

If you have chosen to use a program other than SPSS to enter data, you will still need to define each variable (field, column) as explained in the sections below. The only task that can be skipped is the first, naming the variables.

Naming and Labeling Variables

When you open SPSS, an empty Data Editor window opens. Imagine that we want to enter data from the first four questions in the PEP customer satisfaction survey, plus the ID number. (Refer to the PEP questionnaire at the end of this chapter.) SPSS requires you to assign each variable a **variable name** that is eight characters in length or less (case is unimportant). We begin with the ID number, which is common practice. To replace the default variable name *var00001* with a more descriptive name:

1 Double-click the variable name *var00001* at the top of the first column in the window, or select any cell in the first column, and from the menus choose:

Data
  Define Variable...

This opens the Define Variable dialog box, as shown in Figure 4.2.

Figure 4.2   Define Variable dialog box

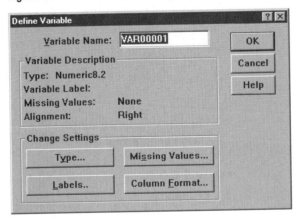

② Type id in place of *var00001* in the Variable Name text box. An ID variable doesn't really need much of a label, but let's see how to add one.

SPSS **variable labels** can be up to 120 characters in length, although most procedures display much less than this maximum value. The label is saved exactly as you type it. These labels are essential because they will be used in place of the short variable name in all SPSS output. The reports and graphics you produce in SPSS will be more effective when the variables have meaningful label.

③ Click Labels in the Define Variable dialog box, which opens the Define Labels dialog box.

④ Type Identification Number in the Variable Label text box, as shown in Figure 4.3.

Figure 4.3   Define Labels dialog box

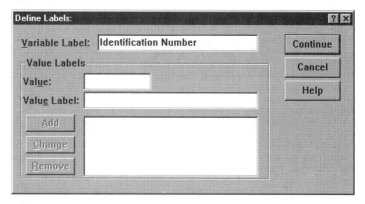

⑤ Click Continue to return to the Define Variable dialog box. Then click the Type pushbutton.

⑥ In the Define Variable Type dialog box, change the 2 to 0 in the Decimal Places text box, then click Continue to return to the main dialog box.

⑦ Click OK to close the Define Variable dialog box.

We now want to define the variable for product type, which records which of two products each respondent owns. Give this variable—that is, the next column in the Data Editor—the name product and the label Product Type by following the same steps as above. Keep the Define Labels dialog box open for the next task.

Labeling Variable Values

A **value label** in SPSS can be up to 60 characters long, although most SPSS output displays only the first 20 characters. Value labels are used to identify individual responses to a question; for example, on a Likert scale, 7 may correspond to a response of *Very satisfied*. For the variable *product*, there are two values to label, 0 (*No response*), 1 (*Fax machine*), and 2 (*Personal copier*). Note that we will code a value (0) that did not appear on the questionnaire to handle missing data caused by a lack of a response.

To add variable labels:

1 Type 0 in the Value text box.

2 Click in the Value Label text box and type No Response.

3 Click Add to store this definition.

4 The cursor returns to the Value text box, and you can go through the same steps to add the other labels. The completed dialog box with all labels is shown in Figure 4.4.

Figure 4.4   Define Labels dialog box for product

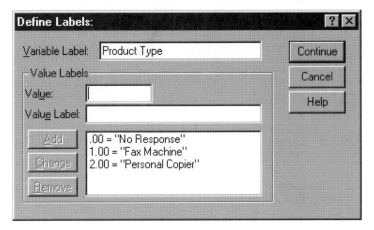

Notice that SPSS has displayed each value with two decimal digits. This is the default display format for numeric data in SPSS, and unless you require this level of accuracy—doubtful for surveys—you should change it. To do so:

5 Click Continue to return to the main dialog box. Then click the Type pushbutton.

⑥ In the Define Variable Type dialog box, change the 2 to 0 in the Decimal Places text box, then click Continue to return to the main dialog box. Notice that information about the variable is displayed in the Variable Description box.

We haven't quite finished defining the product type variable, as missing values must still be specified.

Defining Missing Values

Missing values are specified in the Define Missing Values dialog box. This box is opened by clicking the Missing Values pushbutton in the main dialog box. There are several options to specify missing values, but the usual choice is to list up to three discrete individual missing values in the text boxes under that selection. The value of 0 is to be defined as missing for *product*, so after opening the dialog box, click Discrete missing values, then type 0 in separate text boxes. The completed dialog box is shown in Figure 4.5.

Figure 4.5   Define Missing Values dialog box for product

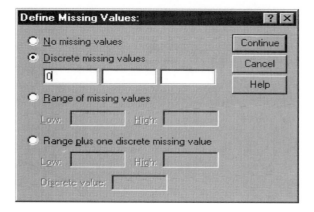

Entering Data

Cases may be entered in any order, since the data can be sorted in SPSS after entry, and because analysis of the data does not depend on case order.

You are now ready to begin entering data (we created the variables *use* and *fail* in the Data Editor). To enter values for the first case—a respondent who owns a fax machine—do the following:

❶ Select the upper left cell in the Data Editor by clicking once on it.

❷ Type 1, the ID for the first case. Then press the Tab key.

③ The highlighted cell has moved to the column for *product*. Type 1, which corresponds to fax machine. Then press the Tab key.

④ The highlighted cell has moved to the column for *use*. Type 5, which corresponds to *Hard to estimate*. Then press the Tab key.

⑤ The highlighted cell is now in the column for *fail*. Type 2, which corresponds to no failure, and then press Enter.

⑥ The cursor goes to the second row, or case, but remains in the same column. To return to the first column for *id*, press Home. You are now ready to enter values for the second respondent. The result at this point is shown in Figure 4.6.

Figure 4.6   Data Editor with values entered for first case

	id	product	use	fail	var	var	v
1	1	1	5	2			
2							
3							
4							

These same steps can be used regardless of how many respondents there are in the sample or how many items there are on the questionnaire.

Since SPSS does not have an automatic backup or save feature for data files, be sure to save your work frequently.

Labeling Multiple Response Variables

As noted above, multiple response items require special attention. Now that we've discussed how to label variables and values in SPSS, we can apply this knowledge to handling multiple response questions.

Labels for Multiple Dichotomy Variables

Recall that multiple dichotomy coding requires creating a variable for each response choice. As a consequence, SPSS uses the variable label to get information on which response was chosen (for example, reads *Time* magazine); thus, the value label codes are not important. So, provide appropriate variable labels for each variable (and you can also label the values of 0 and 1 as *No* and *Yes*, but it is not required).

Labels for Multiple Response Variables

In this type of coding scheme, there are only as many variables as the maximum number of choices; consequently, SPSS gets the necessary information from the value labels, and the variable labels are not important. So, here, make sure that each multiple response variable has a complete set of value labels for all possible choices (and you can give any variable labels you wish to the variables).

Variable Templates

SPSS has other facilities for editing and labeling data, such as the **template**, which provides a method for creating variable definition information and applying it to one or more variables. Templates are useful for variables that share the same labels or missing value specifications, such as Likert scales. We encourage you to explore this feature.

Creating a Codebook

After an SPSS data file has been created, it often is helpful to have a **codebook** for future reference. A codebook contains variable definition information in a concise format—essentially all of the specifications that we entered for each question before we began entering the data. Our small data file now contains only two variables, but you can still display a sample codebook.

To create a codebook, from the menus choose:

Utilities
  File Info

Figure 4.7 displays the result of this choice.

Figure 4.7   File information in Output Navigator

```
            List of variables on the working file

Name                                                              Position

ID         Identification Number                                     1
           Print Format: F8
           Write Format: F8

PRODUCT    Product Type                                              2
           Print Format: F8
           Write Format: F8
           Missing Values: 0

           Value     Label

               0 M   No Response
               1     Fax Machine
               2     Personal Copier

USE        Frequency of use                                          3
           Print Format: F8
           Write Format: F8

           Value     Label

               1     Don't use
               2     Less than once a week
               3     At least once a week
               4     At least once a day
               5     Hard to estimate

FAIL       Did product ever fail to operate                          4
```

The *M* listed next to the values of 0 and 5 for *product* indicate that those two values have been defined as missing. The variable and value labels are all listed, plus the formats for each variable.

To print this information, from the menus choose:

File
  Print...

You may want to keep a hard copy on hand and distribute copies to colleagues.

Accessing Variable Information in SPSS

A codebook is wonderful, but SPSS also provides a facility to let you view variable definition information online, one variable at a time, while you are working with a file.

To access variable information, from the menus choose:

Utilities
 Variables...

You'll see the same information as before but in a different format. Use either of these two codebooks, whichever is most convenient for the task at hand.

What's Next?

You are almost ready for data analysis! Now that you've created a questionnaire, defined a sample, mailed the questionnaire, and entered the data, most of the tedious work of conducting a survey is behind you. However, before data analysis can begin, you need to look for data entry errors and conduct other quality checks. We'll discuss this initial examination of the data in Chapter 5.

1995 PEP Customer Survey

Product Information

Unless indicated otherwise, please circle the appropriate response.

1. Which of these PEP products do you own?

Fax machine	1
Personal copier	2

2. How often do you use your product?
(Circle only one)

Don't use	1
Less than once a week	2
At least once a week	3
At least once a day	4
Hard to estimate	5

3. Did your product ever fail to operate and require repairs?

Yes	1
No *(Skip to question 7)*	2

4. Did you contact PEP because of this failure?

No	1
Yes	2

5. Who repaired your product?

PEP	1
PEP authorized service center	2
Independent service center	3
Other _____	

6. Was the product repaired satisfactorily?

No	1
Yes	2

Product Evaluation

7. Please rate your overall satisfaction with your product.

Very dissatisfied	1
Dissatisfied	2
Satisfied	3
Very satisfied	4

8. Would you buy another PEP product?

No	1
Yes	2

5 Examining Data

By this stage in the survey process, you have completed most of the meticulous and time-consuming tasks. You have an SPSS data file with labels, missing value codes, and formats for each variable. However, at this stage, you shouldn't rush into full-blown data analysis, despite the temptation to analyze all of the potential interesting relationships your file may contain. This chapter discusses several common actions to take before you begin to analyze the data. These can include checking for errors in the file, comparing the respondents to the nonrespondents or to the population to test for bias, checking for the amount and patterns of missing data, transforming one or more variables to create more usable versions, and searching for anything that seems unusual or noteworthy about the data.

Error Checking

As discussed in Chapter 3, there are both sampling and nonsampling errors in survey data, and the latter are generally greater. Some of the nonsampling errors involve respondents mismarking answers, coders miscoding a response, and data entry personnel making errors when creating the data file. Fortunately, many of these errors can be located and corrected by the use of a few simple procedures in SPSS.

Out-of-Range Values

Perhaps the first action to take after the data file is created is to look at the distribution of each variable. As you review each question's responses, look for values that are outside the minimum and maximum values. The SPSS Frequencies procedure is the best choice for this task.

To run the Frequencies procedure, from the menus choose:

Statistics
  Summarize ▶
    Frequencies...

This opens the Frequencies dialog box, as shown in Figure 5.1. You can place all of the categorical variables in the Variable(s) list at one time or review them in groups. Four variables have been selected in Figure 5.1.

Figure 5.1   Frequencies dialog box

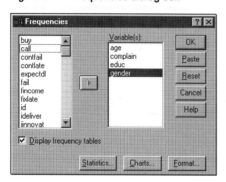

Click OK to run this request; the SPSS Output Navigator opens with the results. The frequency table for *age* is shown in Figure 5.2. The respondents were asked their ages in broad categories and only five responses were valid. As you review this table, look for any values that are outside the accepted range. The actual numeric codes for *age* are 1, 2, 3, 4, and 5, but they don't appear in the table because each category is labeled.

Figure 5.2   Frequency table for age

Age of respondent

		Frequency	Percent	Valid Percent	Cumulative Percent
Valid	20-29	81	13.4	13.4	13.4
	30-39	132	21.8	21.9	35.3
	40-49	186	30.7	30.8	66.2
	50-59	123	20.3	20.4	86.6
	60+	81	13.4	13.4	100.0
	Total	603	99.7	100.0	
Missing	9	2	.3		
	Total	2	.3		
Total		605	100.0		

Only codes in the five valid categories for *age* are listed, plus the *Missing* category for those who didn't answer this question. You should also review the number of responses in each category to see if it makes sense. For example, 13.4% of the valid responses—excluding the two missing cases—are in the *20–29* and *60+* age groups.

Figure 5.3 shows the frequency table for *complain.* The respondents were asked whether or not they were satisfied with complaint resolution.

Figure 5.3   Frequency table for complain

Performance: Complaint Resolution

		Frequency	Percent	Valid Percent	Cumulative Percent
Valid	1	24	4.0	4.1	4.1
	2	19	3.1	3.3	7.4
	3	50	8.3	8.6	16.0
	4	51	8.4	8.8	24.8
	5	95	15.7	16.4	41.2
	6	191	31.6	32.9	74.1
	7	147	24.3	25.3	99.5
	10	3	.5	.5	100.0
	Total	580	95.9	100.0	
Missing	No Answer	11	1.8		
	Don't Know	14	2.3		
	Total	25	4.1		
Total		605	100.0		

Satisfaction was measured on a seven-point scale, but the table shows the value 10 listed as well, which is an error. Three cases were coded with that response. These errors were most probably introduced in data entry because the respondents couldn't select a response coded as 10 on the questionnaire. There are also 25 responses coded as missing, distributed between *No Answer* and *Don't Know.*

When errors are found, you should try to correct them. In this instance, you need to identify which respondents were coded with 10. To identify them, when the number of errors is small, you can search directly in the Data Editor. When there are more errors, you can use SPSS procedures to create output that lists the value of *id* plus the variable being checked. You'll see how to do this in the following section.

Locating Cases with Errors

The first step in isolating cases with errors is to tell SPSS to focus only on those cases. You do this with the Select Cases procedure, accessed from the Data menu. In the Select Cases dialog box, click If condition is satisfied and then click If. This opens the Select Cases If dialog box, as shown in Figure 5.4.

Figure 5.4   Select Cases If dialog box

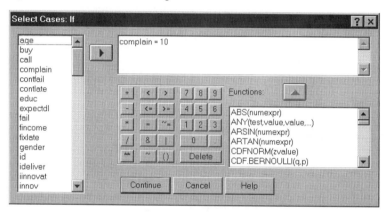

When cases are selected, SPSS creates a filter variable, filter_$, to indicate the filter status. Selected cases have a value of 1; filtered cases have a value of 0. Filtered cases are also indicated with a slash through the row number in the Data Editor.

This dialog box is used to define a subgroup of respondents on which SPSS will perform analyses, until you specify otherwise. You must define a conditional expression in the text box. In this instance, the necessary expression is complain=10, which is evaluated for each case. When true, the case is selected. When not true, the case is filtered out (although not removed from the file). Once you click Continue and then OK in the main dialog box, SPSS will filter out all cases except those with incorrect codes for complaint satisfaction.

The next step is to use one of the reporting procedures in SPSS to list the problem cases. The best choice is typically the Summarize procedure, which produces summary statistics for subgroups but can also list the values of individual variables.

To run the Summarize procedure, from the menus choose:

Statistics
  Summarize ▶
    Case Summaries...

In the Summarize Cases dialog box, move the variables *id* and *complain* to the Variable(s) list and deselect Limit cases to first 100, as shown in Figure 5.5. You want to find all of the cases with errors.

Figure 5.5   Summarize Cases dialog box

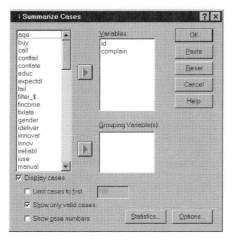

Once you run the procedure, the Output Navigator displays the results, as shown in Figure 5.6.

Figure 5.6   Cases with coding errors for complain

Case Summaries

		ID	Performance: Complaint Resolution
1		9	10
2		181	10
3		224	10
Total	N	3	3

To find the cases to correct in the Data Editor, choose Find from the Edit menu to search for specific data values.

Recall from Figure 5.3 that there were three cases with errors. Now you can easily see that these cases have *id* values of 9, 181, and 224.

The next step is to locate the questionnaires for these cases and correct the errors (in this instance, we found that the respondents chose 1 but the data entry clerk typed 10). After the correct values have been found, you can use the Data Editor to enter them in the appropriate fields.

Backup of Data

When you begin to modify the data is the time when you should also begin to make backup copies of the SPSS data file on tape or disk. Backing up files of all types has become routine, and data files are normally the most critical to archive. There are two primary reasons:

- A copy of the SPSS data file will still be available if your computer's hard disk crashes.

- Changes to the file can be undone if you later decide that the data modifications were unwarranted or unnecessary.

Consistency Errors

Other errors in the data can't be spotted with a frequency table. When a question doesn't apply to some respondents—for example, in a survey about medical procedures, no female should report having received a prostate examination—it should be given a missing code (and the label *Not applicable*). SPSS can help you find situations where respondents answered a question for which they were ineligible, or when codes were entered incorrectly with the same effect. You can use either the Select Cases procedure or the Crosstabs procedure.

With Crosstabs (see Chapter 6), you can create a table that displays the joint distribution of both variables. This makes it easy to see whether any cases fall into cells that should be empty. Here, Select Cases is used because it allows you to locate the problem cases.

To use Select Cases, you must first define the condition that leads to inconsistent responses. In the PEP data, several paired questions ask about specific problems that customers encountered and then whether or not the customer contacted PEP to have the problem resolved. For example, customers were asked whether the product(s) they purchased had ever failed (*fail*) and, if so, whether they contacted the company (*contfail*). Only those who reported that a product had failed (responded *yes* to the first question) should answer the second question. A logical condition can be defined in Select Cases to select those who responded *no* to *fail* but gave a valid response to *contfail*. The expression to make this selection in SPSS is fail=2 and (contfail=1 or contfail=2). In other words, if there was no problem, the customer shouldn't have answered the second question.

After filtering out the respondents with Select Cases and using the Summarize procedure to create a case listing, the output shown in Figure 5.7 is produced. Two respondents have inconsistent codes for the question pair of *fail/contfail*, cases 42 and 473. Both said that their product didn't fail, but they contacted PEP anyway because of a failure.

Figure 5.7   Cases with inconsistent codes

Case Summaries

		ID	Did product ever fail to operate?	Did R contact us because of problem?
1		42	No	Yes
2		473	No	Yes
Total	N	2	2	2

As before, the next step is to review the questionnaire for each respondent. The correction here might seem self-evident (code *contfail* with the value for *not applicable*), but that's not necessarily true. You might find that respondent 42 did have a product that failed (because of extensive comments he or she made on the questionnaire), so the error was in responding *no* to the first question. But at other times, as with a prostate exam for a female, the correction will be obvious.

Missing Data

Every survey you do will have missing data for several questions, so the existence of missing data is not a concern. But too much missing data may indicate a problem with a question, either because of a misunderstanding by the respondents or a poorly written question. Looking for missing data on one question is straightforward using the Frequencies procedure.

There can be other patterns of missing data that are more interesting but also potentially more damaging to the analysis. Survey researchers try to determine whether data is missing at random (often labeled *MCAR*), or whether some respondents have more missing data than others, either on the whole or for only certain questions.

Looking for patterns can be a big job, but it's not difficult to look for one class of problem. Some respondents may have failed to answer most questions, often because they completed the questionnaire hurriedly (a common problem for self-administered surveys). If there is enough missing data, it's often best to discard a respondent from the data file. There are no hard-and-fast rules about how much missing data is too much, so you'll have to make your own decisions.

Counting Missing Data

The SPSS Count procedure, accessed from the Transform menu, counts the number of times a value (or values) occurs among a group of one or more variables for each case. It can count missing values as well. The Count Values within Cases dialog box is shown in Figure 5.8.

Figure 5.8   Count Values within Cases dialog box

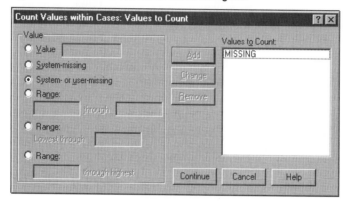

The MISSING selection is used to count both the user- and system-missing values. Count puts the result into a new variable in the Data Editor. For this example, we requested a count of missing values on 13 important variables that ask for the importance and rating of key product attributes (such as reliability and problem resolution).

After you run the Count procedure, use Frequencies to display the amount of missing data for the variables you selected. In Figure 5.9, notice that the count for the category 0.00 is 392 respondents. This means that 392 respondents had no missing values for the 13 questions; in other words, these 392 respondents provided a valid answer for all of the questions.

Figure 5.9   Frequency table for missing data

Missing Data Count

		Frequency	Percent	Valid Percent	Cumulative Percent
Valid	.00	392	64.8	64.8	64.8
	1.00	93	15.4	15.4	80.2
	2.00	78	12.9	12.9	93.1
	3.00	38	6.3	6.3	99.3
	4.00	4	.7	.7	100.0
	Total	605	100.0	100.0	
Total		605	100.0		

To drop cases, select Deleted in the Select Cases dialog box after defining criteria to select the cases you want to retain.

There are many customers who didn't answer each question (605 – 373, or 213), but missing data is common in surveys, and the total amount of it here is not too problematic. However, there are four people who had four missing responses for the 13 questions. This is where your judgment is necessary. Is four missing values too many? Does it indicate that these respondents were so uninterested in the survey, or so distracted, that you shouldn't use them in the analysis?

You already know how to identify these customers if you wish to investigate the matter further (use **Select Cases** or choose **Find** from the Edit menu in the Data Editor to isolate these respondents, get their identification numbers, and carry the analysis further).

Nonresponse Analysis

The potential problem caused by nonresponse was discussed extensively in Chapter 3. Even with relatively high response rates, your data set may be biased, but how can you discover the problem? Generally, there are two approaches. If you know the characteristics of the population, you can compare population values to those of the respondents. Or, if you know something about the nonrespondents, you can compare them to the respondents.

It is common for companies surveying customers, organizations surveying members, or hospitals surveying patients to know some general facts about their population. The PEP company knows, from sales figures, that 70% of its sales are for fax machines and 30% are for personal copiers. In this data set, they found that 77.5% of the customers own a fax machine and 22.5% own a copier, and they want to see whether these proportions are within the limits of sampling error. If, instead, there seems to be a greater response from one type of customer than another, and if the difference is large enough, some changes may need to be made in future surveys.

Testing for Differential Response

The SPSS Chi-Square Test procedure, accessed from Nonparametric Tests on the Statistics menu, tests whether the frequency distribution of a variable in the data file is likely to be equivalent—statistically speaking—to a distribution you specify. The completed dialog box to test the variable *product* is shown in Figure 5.10.

Figure 5.10   Chi-Square Test dialog box

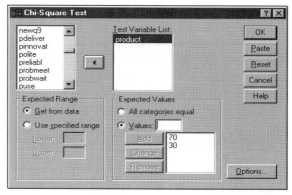

After naming the variable to test, you need to specify the population distribution in the Expected Values text box. The best way to do this is to use the percentages of the categories in the population (make sure they add to 100%). After you click OK, SPSS produces the output shown in Figure 5.11.

Figure 5.11   Chi-square one-sample test for product

Product Type

	Observed N	Expected N	Residual
Fax Machine	469	423.5	45.5
Personal Copier	136	181.5	-45.5
Total	605		

Test Statistics

	Product Type
Chi-Square [1]	16.295
df	1
Asymp. Sig.	.000

1. 0 cells (.0%) have expected frequencies less than 5. The minimum expected cell frequency is 181.5.

The output from the test is shown side-by-side here, but in the Output Navigator the Test Statistics table will appear under the first table (labeled here with the variable label of the variable being tested).

The first table shows the observed frequency distribution for the product type, the expected distribution, given the 70/30 split derived from sales figures, and the residual, or difference, between the expected and observed counts. The residual is then used to calculate a chi-square test statistic and its observed significance.

Every statistical test in SPSS has an explicit or implied **null hypothesis**, which is a statement that usually specifies that there is no relationship between variables or no difference between two or more groups. In this instance, the null hypothesis is that the distribution of *product* in the data file matches that in the total customer base.

The significance, or probability, of a test is the likelihood that you would find the difference that you do (or one larger) between the observed and expected values, given that the null hypothesis is true. In other words, the significance is the likelihood that the differences between the observed and expected counts are caused by sampling variation. The significance reported by SPSS is 0.000 (the value is rounded and is actually less than 0.0005), so the probability that the null hypothesis is correct is very small. Therefore, you can reject the null hypothesis and conclude that there is a differential response between owners of fax machines and personal copiers, so that owners of fax machines are overrepresented.

This test can be applied to any categorical variable and is most frequently used for demographic variables to compare age, gender, and income distributions between the sample and the population. When differences are found, it is possible to weight the data to modify the sample distribution so that it matches the known population values. Although this topic is beyond the scope of this text, weighting is important when response differences are found and when you wish to provide estimates for the total population, such as the total percentage of customers with problems, by combining all groups.

Grouping Categories

Most of the variables in surveys are categorical, either nominal or ordinal in scale. Analysis on such variables is best done when each category has more than a handful of cases, for both statistical and reporting purposes. SPSS provides several transformation procedures that allow you to collapse or group categories so that a sufficient number of cases is in each category.

It is usually not necessary to recode categories when you run tests for mean differences, regression analysis, or other techniques assuming interval or ratio data.

When you examine the distributions for each of the variables to look for incorrect values, you should also be searching for categories where the count is small. It is difficult to specify how many cases is too few because it also depends on the total number of respondents and the total number of response categories. Nevertheless, if any category has less than 15 or so cases, you should consider grouping as an option. It's essential to note that any categories of a nominal variable can be combined (you could combine respondents from the east and west sales regions), but only adjacent categories of ordinal variables can be combined (to maintain the rank order of an ordinal scale).

Figure 5.12 shows the frequency table for the variable *preliabl*, which measures the respondent's rating of product reliability on a scale of 1 to 7. Most respondents rated reliability quite highly, as either a 6 or 7 (for this example, we labeled only the endpoints of *preliabl* so that the other numeric codes are visible). There were only a few responses in the other five categories, so for purposes of analysis and display, it is probably better to combine these categories into one group.

Figure 5.12   Frequency table for preliabl

Performance: Reliability

		Frequency	Percent	Valid Percent	Cumulative Percent
Valid	Not very Reliable	17	2.8	3.1	3.1
	2	6	1.0	1.1	4.2
	3	9	1.5	1.6	5.8
	4	5	.8	.9	6.7
	5	7	1.2	1.3	8.0
	6	146	24.1	26.6	34.6
	Very Reliable	359	59.3	65.4	100.0
	Total	549	90.7	100.0	
Missing	No Answer	23	3.8		
	Don't Know	33	5.5		
	Total	56	9.3		
Total		605	100.0		

Recode

The SPSS Recode procedure is normally the choice for combining the categories of one variable. Since the data will be modified by this procedure, it is usually best to create a new variable rather than recode an existing variable.

To select this transformation, from the menus choose:

Transform
  Recode ▶
    Into Different Variables...

You will need to specify a new variable name and give it a label. Call the new variable *nreliabl* and give it the label *Recoded Reliability Rating*. Then, click Old and New Values to open the Old and New Values dialog box, as shown in Figure 5.13.

Figure 5.13   Old and New Values dialog box

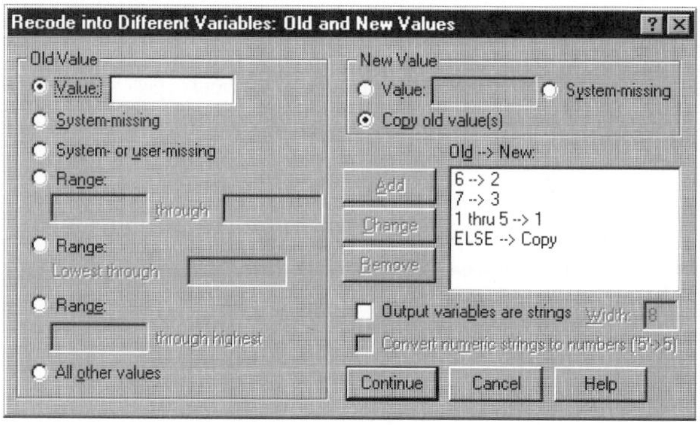

The first five values have been grouped together into the value 1, and the values 6 and 7 have been changed to 2 and 3, respectively. This was done to keep the categories numbered consecutively and to maintain the rank order. All other values and Copy old values are selected to copy the values 8 and 9 for *No Answer* and *Don't Know*, respectively, to the new variable.

When you recode into a new variable, SPSS does not carry along any labels or, more critically, missing value specifications. To make this explicit, Figure 5.14 shows the frequency distribution for the new variable *nreliabl* after the recoding is completed.

Figure 5.14   Frequency table for nreliabl

Recoded Reliability Rating

		Frequency	Percent	Valid Percent	Cumulative Percent
Valid	1	44	7.3	7.3	7.3
	2	146	24.1	24.1	31.4
	3	359	59.3	59.3	90.7
	8	23	3.8	3.8	94.5
	9	33	5.5	5.5	100.0
	Total	605	100.0	100.0	
Total		605	100.0		

There are now only five categories, with 44 respondents in category 1 (verify that this number corresponds to the number of cases in categories 1 through 5 for *preliabl*). The values 8 and 9 were carried to the new variable as requested, but they are no longer labeled or treated as missing data. Whenever you recode a variable, use the Data menu in the Data Editor to label and provide missing value specifications for the new variable, and probably to change the format, since new numeric variables are displayed with two decimal digits, which is too many for categorical data. Analysis and reporting can now proceed with *nreliabl* instead of *preliabl* (you'll see this in Chapter 6).

Creating Scales

Before combining two or more items, it is common to use factor analysis to determine whether the items all seem to measure one underlying attitude. Factor analysis is discussed in Chapter 10.

Many variables in survey research are measured on ordinal scales of 1 to 5, 1 to 7, or 1 to 10. It is common to use these response scales to measure a respondent's rating of various service and product attributes. Moreover, often more than one item is used to evaluate a general topic; for example, a hospital might ask separate questions about the visual appearance, cleanliness, and decor of patient rooms. Each question can be examined separately, but the questions can also be combined to create an overall patient rating of the physical condition of the hospital that is more reliable than any one item.

There are many possible ways to combine items, but the simplest is to add them together when each is measured on the same response scale that runs in the same direction; that is, low numeric codes consistently mean a more negative (or positive) evaluation. Only questions that are ordinal or interval should be combined in this fashion.

Although there is an overall measure of satisfaction on the questionnaire for PEP, let's create another measure composed of three items: reliability (*preliabl* in its original seven-point scale), quality (*qual*), and good value for the money (*value*). Since the original scale runs from 1 to 7, the new variable can take on values from a minimum of 3 (1 + 1 + 1) to a maximum of 21 (7 + 7 + 7).

The SPSS Compute procedure, accessed from the Transform menu, can sum variables, among many other options. The Compute procedure should be thought of as creating new information based on the equivalent of a mathematical equation, with the additional features that you can modify string variables and selectively compute values for subsets of cases rather than the whole file.

Compute

Figure 5.15 shows the Compute Variable dialog box. You must specify a target variable (here, *ovsatis* for overall satisfaction), provide a label if you wish, and then specify the appropriate mathematical expression in the Numeric Expression text box. You can either type directly in the box or use the variable list and calculator pad to create the expression.

When variables are added together, SPSS will, by default, place a system-missing value in the new variable for any respondent who has missing data for one or more of the variables in the expression. This means that the number of valid cases for *ovsatis* will be lower than for any one of the three variables used to create it. This is one of many reasons why you try to have as little missing data as possible in a data file. If there are a lot of missing data, it may not be possible to use the new variable.

Instead of summing the variables, Compute can calculate the mean. The benefit is that the new variable is measured on the same scale as the original variables, but both techniques normally yield the same result in later analysis.

Figure 5.15   Compute Variable dialog box

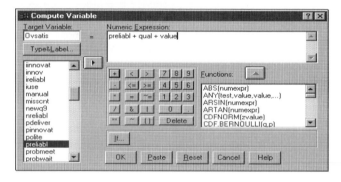

After you click OK, SPSS creates the new variable and places it in the last column in the Data Editor. The next step is to check the frequency distribution of *ovsatis*. Figure 5.16 shows the result.

Figure 5.16   Frequency table for ovsatis

Overall Satisfaction Based on Three Items

		Frequency	Percent	Valid Percent	Cumulative Percent
Valid	4.00	2	.3	.4	.4
	8.00	5	.8	.9	1.3
	9.00	9	1.5	1.7	3.0
	10.00	2	.3	.4	3.4
	11.00	2	.3	.4	3.7
	12.00	3	.5	.6	4.3
	13.00	10	1.7	1.9	6.1
	14.00	11	1.8	2.0	8.2
	15.00	30	5.0	5.6	13.8
	16.00	39	6.4	7.3	21.0
	17.00	45	7.4	8.4	29.4
	18.00	63	10.4	11.7	41.2
	19.00	98	16.2	18.2	59.4
	20.00	97	16.0	18.1	77.5
	21.00	121	20.0	22.5	100.0
	Total	537	88.8	100.0	
Missing	System Missing	68	11.2		
	Total	68	11.2		
Total		605	100.0		

Most respondents rated reliability, value, and quality highly, since over 40% of the valid cases fall into categories 20 and 21. Very few cases are in categories below 12, which is equivalent to an average score of 4—the midpoint—on each item (because $4 + 4 + 4 = 12$). Note that 68 (11%) of the cases had missing data for at least one of the three original variables. You can use *ovsatis* as a new measure of satisfaction in place of or in addition to the overall satisfaction question. For categorical data analysis, it would be best, as you learned above, to group the categories of *ovsatis* by using Recode so that each category has more than a handful of cases.

Beginning the Analysis

Before you begin to analyze the data, there are a few issues to be aware of. First, this chapter has focused on only the most typical data-checking and examination procedures. There are many others, and as you become a more experienced researcher, you'll undoubtedly add a few more techniques to your standard data-checking routine. There may be such a thing as excessive examination of the data, but it's better to err on the side of excess here (if only doctors said the same for our favorite foods). Second, you should always look for data errors, for values that should be grouped, and for other transformations that might be made to the data during the analysis. The only time it's too late is when the final report has been printed.

Given these concerns, you're now ready to analyze the data. The remaining chapters will explore common techniques for analyzing and displaying categorical data and then discuss more advanced techniques for scales and interval and ratio data.

6 Analyzing Categorical Data

Data analysis is different from other phases of the survey process in that it cannot easily be reduced to a formula or a series of steps.

You can begin data analysis with any variable or any technique that you want. The appropriate technique depends on the scale of measurement (nominal, ordinal, interval, or ratio), the goal of your analysis, and your comfort level in using the techniques and interpreting the results.

Any of the SPSS data analysis procedures can be used to analyze survey data. However, in data analysis, it is best to proceed from the simple to the complex. In Chapter 5, for example, we began by examining the responses to individual questions. This chapter discusses techniques for analyzing nominal or ordinal categorical data, focusing on crosstabulations of two or three variables. Subsequent chapters will discuss more complex analytical techniques, such as regression and factor analysis. The best approach is to make sure that you understand your data fully before you begin your analysis. Then, you can interpret the output from higher-level statistical procedures with more confidence and accuracy.

Frequencies and Charts

In Chapter 5, you learned how to check for errors in a data file by using the Frequencies procedure. This section begins with another look at Frequencies and one of its options. A critical question on the Personal Electronic Products (PEP) survey asked whether the customer was willing to buy another product from PEP. To examine the distribution of this variable and to display the results graphically, open the Frequencies dialog box and move *buy* into the Variable(s) list. Click Charts to open the Frequencies Charts dialog box, as shown in Figure 6.1.

Figure 6.1   Frequencies Charts dialog box

This dialog box allows you to request either a bar chart or histogram for the selected variable. A bar chart, which displays a separate bar for each category of a variable proportional to the count or percentage of cases in that category, is appropriate for nominal or ordinal data. The variable *buy* is measured on only a five-point scale, from *Not at all Likely* to *Extremely Likely*, so it's ordinal in scale. Select Bar chart(s) to request the bar chart, and select Percentages to label the axis with percentages (displaying percentages is a better choice than counts). Click Continue and then OK to produce the frequency table shown in Figure 6.2.

Figure 6.2   Frequency table for variable buy

Willingness to Buy Product Again

		Frequency	Percent	Valid Percent	Cumulative Percent
Valid	Not at all Likely	20	3.3	3.7	3.7
	Not Very Likely	63	10.4	11.5	15.2
	Somewhat Likely	110	18.2	20.1	35.3
	Very Likely	195	32.2	35.6	70.9
	Extremely Likely	159	26.3	29.1	100.0
	Total	547	90.4	100.0	
Missing	No Answer	37	6.1		
	Don't Know	21	3.5		
	Total	58	9.6		
Total		605	100.0		

Approximately 90% of the respondents answered this question, which is not too surprising for a question about future behavior. As mentioned in Chapter 2, answers to questions about future behavior should be treated as approximations (which is another good reason to treat *buy* as an ordinal variable). It is reassuring to PEP that approximately 64% of the responses were either *Very Likely* or *Extremely Likely*.

The bar chart, as shown in Figure 6.3, is displayed right below the frequency table in the Output Navigator.

Figure 6.3   Bar chart for variable buy

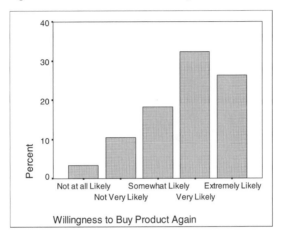

Pie charts are another way to display categorical data. You can use the SPSS Chart Editor to change a bar chart into a pie chart:

1. Double-click the bar chart to place it in a Chart Editor window. In this window, you can edit the chart and save it in several common formats for use in other programs.

2. Choose Pie from the Gallery menu. This opens the Pie Charts dialog box, as shown in Figure 6.4.

Figure 6.4   Pie Charts dialog box

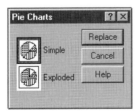

To create a simple pie chart, click the Simple icon and then click Replace. This changes the bar chart into a pie chart, as shown in Figure 6.5.

Figure 6.5   Pie chart for variable buy

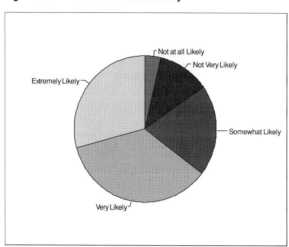

The pie chart clearly displays how a majority of customers are either *Extremely Likely* or *Very Likely* to buy from PEP again.

Pareto Charts

Another type of bar chart—a Pareto chart—is an excellent way to display categorical data and make it easy to see which categories contain the most responses. To produce a Pareto chart, choose **Pareto** from the Graphs menu. This opens the Pareto Charts dialog box, as shown in Figure 6.6.

Figure 6.6   Pareto Charts dialog box

Select the chart type

Select the type of data to be used to create the chart

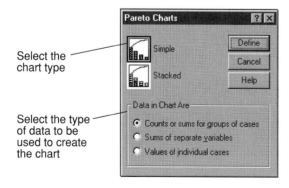

You will encounter the features of this dialog box repeatedly with various types of graphs. You generally have two decisions to make. The first is the type of chart to create. For example, a Pareto chart can be a simple chart or a stacked chart, which displays frequencies of one variable within categories of a second. Second, you must tell SPSS whether the data used to create the chart are for groups of cases (the default), separate variables, or individual cases. In this instance, since each bar will be for groups of cases (for example, those who said *Very Likely*), you can accept the defaults and click Define.

Next, you have to tell SPSS which variable to display. In this example, we'll switch to the variable *pinnovat*, which measures, on a seven-point scale, whether the respondent believes that PEP is an innovative company. This variable must be moved into the Category Axis text box. Additionally, some charts display missing values unless you tell SPSS otherwise. To turn off their display, click Options and then select Display groups defined by missing values. (This is a general approach for any type of graph.) The resulting Pareto chart is shown in Figure 6.7.

Figure 6.7   Pareto chart for variable pinnovat

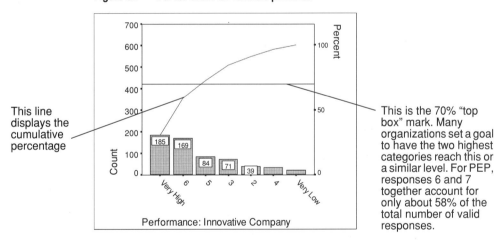

This line displays the cumulative percentage

This is the 70% "top box" mark. Many organizations set a goal to have the two highest categories reach this or a similar level. For PEP, responses 6 and 7 together account for only about 58% of the total number of valid responses.

Notice that the categories of *pinnovat* are displayed in order, from left to right, on the basis of the frequency of each category. You can immediately see that category 7 (*Very High* level of innovation) was chosen most often, followed by categories 6 and 5. However, the midpoint, category 4, is not next; instead, categories 3 and 2 follow, then 4, and finally 1 (*Very Low* level of innovation). The cumulative percentage line is added automatically by SPSS. For this example, we've added the reference line, which is accessed from the Chart menu in the Chart Editor.

Crosstabulations

Many researchers consider crosstabulations the core of survey data analysis because so much survey data is nominal or ordinal. Crosstabulations display the joint distribution of two or more categorical variables. For a two-variable table, each (valid) category of one variable forms a row, and the categories of the second variable form the columns. If there are three or more variables, SPSS can produce separate tables for each category of the additional variables.

It is often sufficient to simply display the relationship between two variables without doing any statistical testing. We'll show you that first. If you want to go further, the Crosstabs procedure tests whether two variables are related (for example, *Are those who own a fax machine more satisfied than those who own a personal copier?*) and measures the strength of the relationship.

Crosstabulations are commonly used to explore how demographic variables are related to various attitudes and behaviors, but they can also be used to see how one attitude is related to another (for example, *Are those with lower overall satisfaction less willing to recommend PEP products?*).

To run the Crosstabs procedure, from the menus choose:

Statistics
  Summarize ▶
    Crosstabs...

This opens the Crosstabs dialog box, as shown in Figure 6.8.

Figure 6.8   Crosstabs dialog box

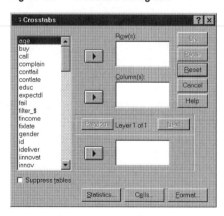

You must specify at least one row variable and one column variable. We'll study the relationship between gender and the reliability rating for the product purchased by the respondent. For this example, reliability (the variable *nreliabl*) is measured in three categories: *Poor, Moderate,* and *Good.* By convention, the demographic variables are usually placed in the column dimension of the table. After selecting the variables, click Cells. This opens the Crosstabs Cell Display dialog box, as shown in Figure 6.9.

Figure 6.9   Crosstabs Cell Display dialog box

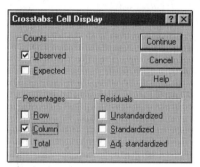

By default, only the observed count—the number of cases in each cell of the table—is displayed. You normally will also want to see percentages, and percentages are based on the independent or predictor variables because it allows comparison of responses across categories of the predictors. In this table, that means basing percentages on *gender*, a demographic variable. Because *gender* defines the columns, select Column in the Percentages group.

The resulting crosstabulation is shown in Figure 6.10. SPSS automatically titles the table so that you know which variables are being displayed together. Each cell contains the count and column percentage (labeled *% of Gender* to make its base explicit). The table also includes row and column totals. Slightly more females than males (67.4% to 61.8%) found their product's reliability to be *Good.* Very few females or males rated the PEP product's reliability as *Poor.*

Figure 6.10   Crosstabulation for gender and reliability

			GENDER		Total
			Male	Female	
Recoded Reliability Rating	Poor	Count	14	30	44
		% of GENDER	7.0%	8.6%	8.0%
	Moderate	Count	62	84	146
		% of GENDER	31.2%	24.0%	26.6%
	Good	Count	123	236	359
		% of GENDER	61.8%	67.4%	65.4%
Total		Count	199	350	549
		% of GENDER	100.0%	100.0%	100.0%

Try to avoid reporting on percentages based on cells with a small number of cases.

This table is adequate for data analysis, and you can see that males and females differ little in their rating of reliability, and that reliability is generally rated highly by PEP customers. But this table is not formatted for inclusion in a report. It needs a new title, a different overall look, and other changes to improve its appearance. The following section discusses how to make these and other changes.

Pivot Tables

Much of the output in SPSS is presented in tables that can be pivoted interactively; that is, using the Pivot Table Editor, you can rearrange rows and columns without rerunning the table. You can also change the width of columns, hide rows and columns, change the nesting order of objects in rows or columns, and make font and formatting changes.

To activate the SPSS Pivot Table Editor, simply double-click the table. If you double-click the table shown in Figure 6.10, it appears in the SPSS Output Navigator as shown in Figure 6.11.

Figure 6.11   Pivot table and pivoting trays for crosstabulation

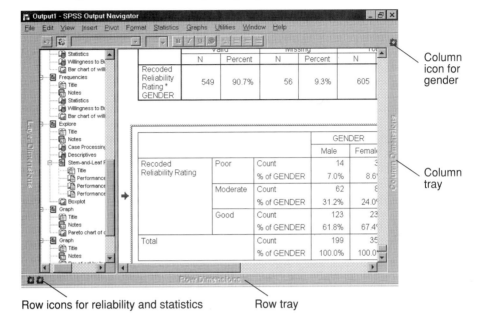

Column icon for gender

Column tray

Row icons for reliability and statistics

Row tray

Three trays appear at the sides of the Output Navigator window, labeled *Row Dimensions*, *Column Dimensions*, and *Layer Dimensions* (the layer dimension is for a third variable, which you will see later). The trays contain icons that represent the variables and statistics displayed in that dimension, in their display order. So, in the row dimension, the icon on the left is for reliability rating, and the icon next to it is for the count and percentage statistics. You can click on an icon with the left mouse button and drag it to any dimension or change the order of icons in a dimension.

The table we'd like to produce will change the nesting order in the row dimension, placing the statistics above the reliability rating. After dragging the statistics icon to the left of the reliability icon, the table switches to the view shown in Figure 6.12 (only the table is displayed, not the full screen).

Figure 6.12   Crosstabulation with reliability nested under statistics

			GENDER		
			Male	Female	Total
Count	Recoded Reliability Rating	Poor	14	30	44
		Moderate	62	84	146
		Good	123	236	359
	Total		199	350	549
% of GENDER	Recoded Reliability Rating	Poor	7.0%	8.6%	8.0%
		Moderate	31.2%	24.0%	26.6%
		Good	61.8%	67.4%	65.4%
	Total		100.0%	100.0%	100.0%

This table is much easier to read, since it separates the counts from the percentages. Several additional modifications (described below) produce the table shown in Figure 6.13.

Figure 6.13   Modified crosstabulation

Relationship of Reliability Rating and Gender

		GENDER		
		Male	Female	Total
Count	Poor	14	30	44
	Moderate	62	84	146
	Good	123	236	359
	Total	199	350	549
% of GENDER	Poor	7.0%	8.6%	8.0%
	Moderate	31.2%	24.0%	26.6%
	Good	61.8%	67.4%	65.4%
	Total	100.0%	100.0%	100.0%

To modify the table as shown:

1. Choose TableLooks from the Format menu and select Times Roman on the TableLook Files list.

2. Choose Title from the Insert menu, double-click the title cell, type the new title, and press Enter.

3. Click the right edge of the statistics column and drag it to the right to increase the width of the column.

4. Click the words *Recoded Reliability Rating* and then press Delete to remove them.

After you've edited the table, click anywhere outside the table in the Output Navigator window, and SPSS will exit the editing mode and return to the normal view. Many more modifications can be made. For example, you can add color to accent certain cells or dimensions, you can change every property of a single cell, you can add footnotes for particular values, and you can include a table caption. You'll see more of the pivot table features toward the end of this chapter.

Clustered Bar Charts

A bar chart graphically displays the same information as a frequency table; a **clustered bar chart** graphically displays the same information as a cross tabulation. For this example, we will create a clustered bar chart for gender and reliability.

From the Graphs menu, choose Bar. Click the Clustered icon and then click Define. This opens the Define Clustered Bar dialog box, as shown in Figure 6.14.

Figure 6.14   Define Clustered Bar dialog box

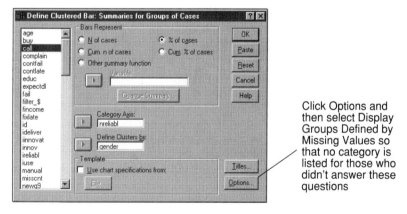

Click Options and then select Display Groups Defined by Missing Values so that no category is listed for those who didn't answer these questions

Move the variable that will define the categories, which is equivalent to the dependent variable or the response variable (*nreliabl*), into the Category Axis text box. Move the demographic variable or independent variable (*gender*) into the Define Clusters by text box. A separate bar will be created for each value of this variable. As with crosstabulations, it is important to use percentages, not counts, so you also select % of cases in the Bars Represent group. This produces the clustered bar chart shown in Figure 6.15.

Figure 6.15   Clustered bar chart for gender and reliability

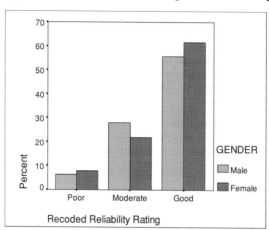

If you compare the percentages in this chart to the crosstabulation in either Figure 6.12 or Figure 6.13, you can see that they are identical. It's also evident that males and females differ little in their rating of reliability.

Testing Relationships

One of the risks in survey research is to forget that all of the distributions you display and all of the statistics you calculate are subject to sampling error (and other errors as well, as discussed in previous chapters). A symptom of this mistake is regarding the percentages in a table as fixed quantities, so that for the crosstabulation we've been investigating, the fact that 67.4% of the females gave reliability a *Good* rating compared to 61.8% of the males means that females think PEP products are more reliable. The existence of sampling error, however, means that these percentages are simply your best estimate of the unknown population values. Furthermore, the sample percentages are unlikely to be exactly equal to the population percentages. Given the existence of sampling error, it is possible that there is actually no difference in the ratings of males and females, even though we found approximately a 6% difference in this sample.

With SPSS, you can test to determine whether sample differences are due to population differences (SPSS was first developed to do exactly this type of testing). The hypothesis that no difference exists in the population is called the null hypothesis.

Each statistical procedure has its own form of such a test. In Crosstabs, the expected count or frequency in each cell of the table is compared to the actual count to calculate a Pearson chi-square statistic. The expected count is the number of cases expected if the null hypothesis is true, which means that, in this instance, the distribution of the response variable is the same for both males and females.

The Strength of a Relationship

Once you know that two variables are related, you should also investigate the strength of the relationship. There are several statistics for nominal or ordinal data that can provide this information. In addition to the strength of a relationship, you need to know whether a relationship is positive or negative; for example, if people with higher incomes think that PEP products are more reliable, that would be a positive relationship because higher values of one variable are associated with higher values of the second variable.

Producing the Statistics

Once you specify which crosstabulation to produce, in the Crosstabs dialog box, click Statistics to open the Crosstabs Statistics dialog box, as shown in Figure 6.16. The statistics available for nominal or ordinal data are listed in separate groups. The chi-square statistic is listed by itself in the upper left corner. The variable *nreliabl* is ordinal, but so is *gender*. As explained in Chapter 2, dichotomous variables can be considered as ordinal.

Ordinal measures of association are based on comparing pairs of cases. Each statistic takes on values between −1 and +1, where a negative sign indicates a negative relationship and a positive sign indicates a positive relationship. We've chosen Somers' *d*, which takes into account which variable is the dependent variable and which is the independent variable. If two variables are unrelated, the values of these ordinal statistics will be 0.

Figure 6.16   Crosstabs Statistics dialog box

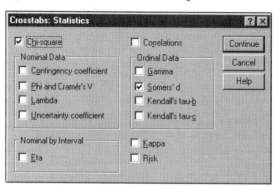

After running the request, SPSS produces the chi-square statistical output shown in Figure 6.17 (we've omitted the crosstabulation here because it has already been displayed). There are three chi-square values listed, but we'll focus on the Pearson value, which is adequate for most analyses. The actual chi-square value of 3.429 is not important to note, nor is the value for degrees of freedom (*df*). SPSS uses these values with the theoretical chi-square distribution to report a **significance level** (labeled *Asymptotic Sig.*). The significance level is 0.180 for the Pearson chi-square, which means that, if the null hypothesis that male and female reliability ratings don't differ is true, you would expect to see a chi-square value at least this large approximately 18 times out of 100 samples. This is reasonably frequent, so you can't reject the null hypothesis. In other words, you have no evidence that there is a difference in attitude between males and females in the population.

Figure 6.17   Chi-square statistics for gender and reliability

Chi-Square Tests

	Value	df	Asymp. Sig. (2-tailed)
Pearson Chi-Square	3.429[1]	2	.180
Likelihood Ratio	3.390	2	.184
Linear-by-Linear Association	.522	1	.470
N of Valid Cases	549		

1. 0 cells (.0%) have expected count less than 5. The minimum expected count is 15.95.

The footnote concerning the number of cells with expected counts less than 5 should be noted. If too many cells have low expected values, it will be necessary to group categories (see Chapter 5).

Even though there is no relationship between the two variables, let's examine the Somers' *d* statistics, as shown in Figure 6.18.

Figure 6.18   Somers' d statistics

Directional Measures

			Value	Asymp. Std. Error[1]	Approx. T[2]	Approx. Sig.
Ordinal Measures	Somers' d	Symmetric	.045	.042	1.078	.281
		Recoded Reliability Rating Dependent	.046	.043	1.078	.281
		GENDER Dependent	.043	.040	1.078	.281

1. Not assuming the null hypothesis
2. Using the asymptotic standard error assuming the null hypothesis.

Often, the 0.05 significance level is used as a criterion to determine whether two variables are associated.

There are three statistics; the one to use is for *Recoded Reliability Rating Dependent*. The value of Somers' *d* is 0.046, which is very close to 0 and slightly positive. It's positive because females, who are coded with 2 on *gender*, are associated more often with responses of 3 (*Good*) on *nreliabl*. Somers' *d*, like the chi-square statistic, has a related significance level. Its significance level of 0.281 means that if Somers' *d* is actually 0 in the population of PEP customers, the chance of finding a value of 0.046 is approximately 28 times out of 100 samples (which is pretty likely). Once again, you have no reason to reject the null hypothesis of no association between the two variables.

Figure 6.19 shows a table where there is a relationship. Here, females (35%) are much more willing than males (19%) to say that they are *Extremely Likely* to buy again from PEP; females also gave fewer responses of *Somewhat Likely*.

Figure 6.19   Crosstabulation for buy and gender

Willingness to Buy Product Again * GENDER Crosstabulation

% of GENDER

		GENDER		Total
		Male	Female	
Willingness to Buy Product Again	Not at all Likely	5.5%	2.6%	3.7%
	Not Very Likely	12.4%	11.0%	11.5%
	Somewhat Likely	24.9%	17.3%	20.1%
	Very Likely	38.3%	34.1%	35.6%
	Extremely Likely	18.9%	35.0%	29.1%
Total		100.0%	100.0%	100.0%

Is this difference statistically significant? The answer is yes, using the output shown in Figure 6.20. The significance level of the chi-square value is 0.001, so there is little chance of finding these percentage differences if there is no difference in the population.

Figure 6.20   Chi-square statistics for gender and buy

Chi-Square Tests

	Value	df	Asymp. Sig. (2-tailed)
Pearson Chi-Square	18.610[1]	4	.001
Likelihood Ratio	19.145	4	.001
Linear-by-Linear Association	12.847	1	.000
N of Valid Cases	547		

1. 0 cells (.0%) have expected count less than 5. The minimum expected count is 7.35.

No cell has an expected value of less than 5, so you can use the chi-square test

What is the strength of the relationship? As you can see in Figure 6.21, the value of Somers' *d,* with willingness to buy PEP products the dependent variable, is 0.188. This is a positive but rather modest value. Females are more willing than males to buy the product again, but the difference is not great. The Somers' *d* value is significantly different from 0, since the significance level is 0.000 (which means that it is actually less than 0.0005).

The SPSS Pivot Table Editor was used to modify this table to show only the relevant information (compare to Figure 6.18). This is another example of how the Pivot Table Editor can improve the reporting of results.

Figure 6.21   Somers' d statistics for gender and buy

Directional Measures

			Value	Asymp. Std.Error[1]	Approx. T[2]	Approx. Sig.
Ordinal Measures	Somers' d	Willingness to Buy Product Again Dependent	.188	.047	3.951	.000

1. Not assuming the null hypothesis
2. Using the asymptotic standard error assuming the null hypothesis.

Three-Variable Crosstabulations

This chapter concludes with a brief look at a three-way crosstabulation. Figure 6.22 shows the table for *gender* by *call* (whether the customer has called a sales rep in the last three months) by *region*.

Figure 6.22   Three-way crosstabulation

Spoke with Sales Rep last 3 months * Region * GENDER Crosstabulation

% of Region

GENDER			Spoke with Sales Rep last 3 months		Total
			Yes	No	
Male	Region	East	6.5%	93.5%	100.0%
		Midwest	**21.2%**	78.8%	100.0%
		South	12.2%	87.8%	100.0%
		Southwest	5.7%	94.3%	100.0%
		West		100.0%	100.0%
	Total		10.0%	90.0%	100.0%
Female	Region	East	13.0%	87.0%	100.0%
		Midwest	4.3%	95.7%	100.0%
		South	**19.8%**	80.2%	100.0%
		Southwest	12.8%	87.2%	100.0%
		West	14.7%	85.3%	100.0%
	Total		13.1%	86.9%	100.0%

This table looked different when it first appeared in the Output Navigator. We've changed the default format of the table using the Pivot Table Editor. Since the table was originally too wide to display easily, we modified its appearance to make it more rectangular by switching the location of *region* and *call*. We also changed the TableLook format to the Times Roman choice. In addition, we used boldface to emphasize the values for the two categories that have the highest *Yes* responses for males and females.

Statistical tests to determine whether there is a relationship between two of the variables can also be requested for such tables, as well as measures for the strength of the relationship. However, the Crosstabs procedure does not produce a chi-square test appropriate for simultaneously testing the three-way relationship. Only separate two-way tables, controlling for the third variable (such as the table for *region* by *call* for males only), can be tested. Three-way relationships can be investigated with loglinear analysis, available in three different advanced procedures in SPSS, the CHAID procedure, or the various procedures in the Categories model.

7 Multiple Response Questions

Multiple response items differ from other questions in several important ways. Although multiple response items are always categorical, they must be treated differently from single response questions. Since the variables created from one multiple response question are, by definition, related, it's logical to display all the responses as one group. This can be difficult to accomplish graphically, so multiple response data are almost invariably displayed in tabular form.

Another important characteristic of multiple response questions is that no statistical tests can be conducted on the group of responses. This is because standard statistical tests assume that the observations in a file are independent, which means that one person's answer to a question doesn't influence another's. But for multiple response items, each person can (and usually does) give more than one answer, and that violates this key assumption. Thus, multiple response items are studied with simple counts and percentages.

The Personal Electronic Products (PEP) company survey, introduced in Chapter 1, contained a question asking where the respondent shopped for electronic products such as fax machines and copiers, with the three possible answers of a consumer electronics, office products, or department store. This is a **multiple response question**; a respondent can select any combination of the three answers. SPSS displays multiple response items with the Multiple Response procedure. The first step in using it is to tell SPSS which variables compose the multiple response grouping, or set. To run this procedure, from the menus choose:

Statistics
  Multiple Response ▶
    Define Sets...

The Define Multiple Response Sets dialog box is shown in Figure 7.1.

Figure 7.1   Define Multiple Response Sets dialog box

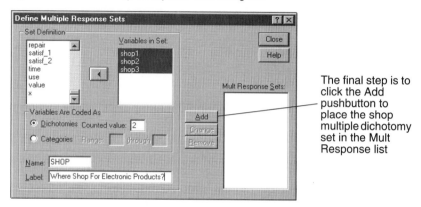

The final step is to click the Add pushbutton to place the shop multiple dichotomy set in the Mult Response list

Select the variables that compose the set (*shop1, shop2,* and *shop3*), and give the new set a name (*shop*) and a label, if you wish. Select **Dichotomies** or **Categories** (for multiple response variables) to specify how the variables are coded, and specify the value or range to use. The shopping variables are coded dichotomously, with a value of 2 indicating *Yes.*

After clicking **Add,** you'll see that the new set name begins with a dollar sign ($), which identifies it as a special variable. (The dollar sign counts as one of the eight allowed characters in a variable name.) When you click **Close,** SPSS stores this information for use in creating a frequency table or a crosstabulation.

Multiple Response Frequencies

To create a frequency table for a multiple response question, from the menus choose:

Statistics
  Multiple Response ▶
    Frequencies...

The Multiple Response Frequencies dialog box is shown in Figure 7.2.

Figure 7.2   Multiple Response Frequencies dialog box

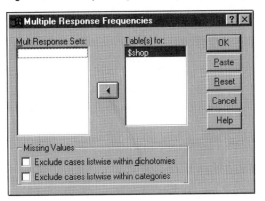

In the Table(s) For list, place the multiple response set or sets for which you are requesting frequency tables, and click OK. SPSS will provide percentages based on both the number of cases and responses. The resulting table is shown in Figure 7.3. As you can see, this output has not yet been converted to the Output Navigator format.

Figure 7.3   Multiple response frequency table for shop1, shop2, and shop3

```
Group $SHOP  Where Shop For Electric Products?
    (Value tabulated = 2)

                                                      Pct of  Pct of
Dichotomy label                      Name     Count  Responses Cases

Shopped in Department Store          SHOP1     445    28.8    73.8
Shopped in Office Product Store      SHOP2     533    34.5    88.4
Shopped In Consumer Electronic Store SHOP3     568    36.7    94.2
                                             -------  -----   -----
                        Total responses       1546   100.0   256.4

2 missing cases;  603 valid cases
```

The *Pct of Cases* column displays percentages based on the 603 people who answered this question. The most common response was shopping in a consumer electronics store, as 568 respondents made this selection, or 94.2% of the valid cases. All three choices were picked by a majority of respondents, with the least frequent being shopping in a department store, at 73.8%. The *Pct of Responses* column displays percentages based on the total number of responses (here, 1546). Shopping in a consumer electronics store comprised 36.7% of all responses. The responses suggest that PEP should keep its fax machines and copiers in all three of these kinds of stores.

Multiple Response Crosstabs

Once you've created one or more multiple response sets, you can also create crosstabulations with these groupings and any of the regular categorical variables or other multiple response variables. Row and/or column percentages can be requested, and these percentages can be based on either the cases or responses. As with regular crosstabulations, you can add a third, or layer, variable to investigate complex relationships.

Figure 7.4 shows the Multiple Response Crosstabs dialog box. We're going to investigate the relationship between income (*fincome*) and the *$shop* multiple response variable, on the theory that economic condition may affect where someone shops.

Figure 7.4   Multiple Response Crosstabs dialog box

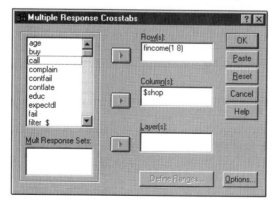

Notice that you must specify the range of values for *fincome*. Click Options to open the Multiple Response Crosstabs Options dialog box, as shown in Figure 7.5.

Figure 7.5   Multiple Response Crosstabs Options dialog box

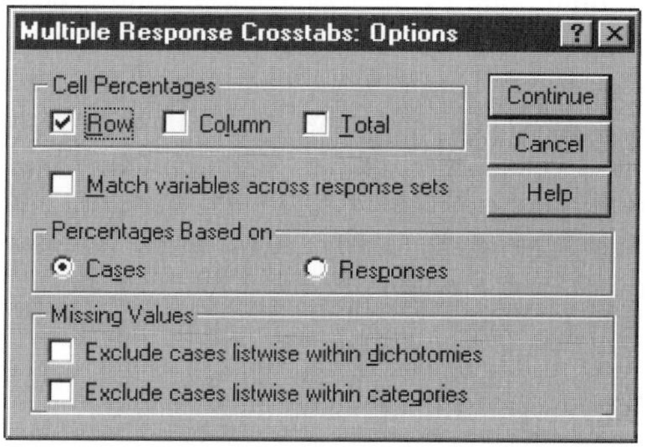

We've selected Row under Cell Percentages, and we've retained the default selection of percentages based on Cases. Click Continue, and then click OK in the main dialog box to produce the crosstabulation shown in Figure 7.6.

Figure 7.6   Multiple response crosstabulation for income and shop

```
                          $SHOP

                 Count  IShopped  Shopped  Shopped
                 Row pct Iin Depar in Offic In Consu   Row
                         Itmen     e Pr     mer       Total
                         ISHOP1    ISHOP2   ISHOP3   I
FINCOME          --------+--------+--------+--------+
                      1  I    38  I    54  I    59  I    64
   Less than $20,000     I  59.4  I  84.4  I  92.2  I  13.5
                         +--------+--------+--------+
                      2  I    32  I    37  I    41  I    43
   $20,000 to $24,999    I  74.4  I  86.0  I  95.3  I   9.1
                         +--------+--------+--------+
                      3  I    74  I    93  I   101  I   103
   $25,000 to $34,999    I  71.8  I  90.3  I  98.1  I  21.8
                         +--------+--------+--------+
                      4  I    79  I    92  I    97  I   101
   $35,000 to $44,999    I  78.2  I  91.1  I  96.0  I  21.4
                         +--------+--------+--------+
                      5  I    37  I    40  I    47  I    49
   $45,000 to $54,999    I  75.5  I  81.6  I  95.9  I  10.4
                         +--------+--------+--------+
                      6  I    33  I    29  I    36  I    38
   $55,000 to $64,999    I  86.8  I  76.3  I  94.7  I   8.0
                         +--------+--------+--------+
                      7  I    19  I    26  I    28  I    28
   $65,000 to $74,999    I  67.9  I  92.9  I 100.0  I   5.9
                         +--------+--------+--------+
                      8  I    34  I    39  I    41  I    47
   $75,000 or more       I  72.3  I  83.0  I  87.2  I   9.9
                         +--------+--------+--------+
                 Column      346      410      450     473
                 Total      73.2     86.7     95.1   100.0

Percents and totals based on respondents
```

The above crosstabulation clearly shows differences by income. Those in the lowest income category are less likely to shop at department stores compared to the other two types. People with incomes between $55,000 and $64,999 were the most likely to shop in department stores, and the least likely to shop in office product stores. Whether these differences are large enough to be important factors in PEP's decision making is a judgment call (remember that you shouldn't do statistical tests with multiple response data).

In cells with a small number of cases, the percentages are necessarily based on those few cases, so you should be cautious in reporting on the results.

The Tables Procedure

The SPSS for Windows Base system, as we've just seen, allows you to analyze and report on multiple response data. SPSS also provides the Tables module, an add-on option that enables you to prepare customized tables suitable for presentation or publication. The SPSS Tables procedure offers more flexibility in presenting multiple response variables. So that you can compare the output from Tables to that obtained using the Multiple Response procedure, we'll create the same basic tables as in the examples above.

The Tables option includes three procedures: Basic Tables, General Tables, and Tables of Frequencies. To report on multiple response items, you should use the General Tables procedure. The main dialog box for General Tables is shown in Figure 7.7.

Figure 7.7   General Tables dialog box

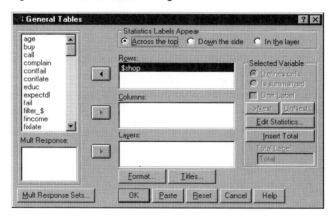

The *$shop* multiple response set must be defined again, and it is done in General Tables almost exactly as it is in the Define Multiple Response Sets procedure; the difference is that you must also choose whether you want to base percentages on cases or responses. Here, the default is retained, which is to base percentages on the number of cases.

To create a frequency table, place the variable *$shop* in the Rows box, and then request statistics by clicking Edit Statistics. By default, Tables produces a count based on the number of respondents. In the cells of a table, this is equivalent to the number of cases.

Figure 7.8   Cell Statistics dialog box for multiple response variable

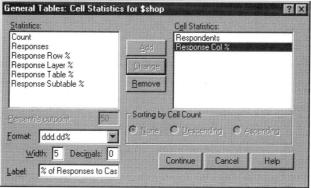

Add Response Col % to the Cell Statistics list to get percentages (which, because of how we previously defined the multiple response set, will be based on cases). Use the Format, Width, and Label options to modify the display characteristics of each statistic. We've changed the label for the column percentage and specified a value of 0 in the Decimals text box so that no decimal digits are displayed.

Back in the main dialog box, click Insert Total to get a total after the frequencies for each choice of store. The table as it first appears in the Output Navigator is shown in Figure 7.9.

Figure 7.9   Frequency table for responses to shop1, shop2, and shop3

		Cases	% of Responses to Cases
Where Shop For Electronic Products	Shopped in Department Store	445	74%
	Shopped in Office Product Store	533	88%
	Shopped In Consumer Electronic Store	568	94%
Total		603	256%

Compare this table to the frequency table shown in Figure 7.3, produced using Multiple Response Frequencies. Tables output, by comparison, is produced in the new Output Navigator and can be modified using the Pivot Table Editor. The percentages in Figure 7.9 print without a decimal digit, as requested.

The Pivot Table Editor was used to create the modified version of the table shown in Figure 7.10.

Figure 7.10   Multiple response table modified with Pivot Table Editor

	Where Customers Shopped for a Copier or Fax Machine			
Columns	Shopped in Department Store	Shopped in Office Product Store	Shopped In Consumer Electronic Store	Total
Cases	445	533	568	603
% of Responses to Cases	74%	88%	94%	256%

We used the Pivot Table Editor to:

1. Transpose the row (the variables) and the column (the statistics).

2. Change the TableLook to the Modern format.

3. Bold the words Cases and % of Responses to Cases and change their point size.

4. Add a new title for the multiple response set and change its point size.

5. Center the numbers in the cells.

6. Change the width of the column for the statistics.

Many more editing options are available, but this example provides an indication of the power and flexibility of the Pivot Table Editor.

Crosstabulations with Tables

Creating the table of income and the shopping multiple response variable—the equivalent of Figure 7.6—is a simple task, so we won't show the Table dialog box selections. Figure 7.11 presents the table as it appears in the Output Navigator.

Figure 7.11   Multiple response crosstabulation of fincome and $shop

| | | Where Shop For Electronic Products? | | | |
		Shopped in Department Store	Shopped in Office Product Store	Shopped In Consumer Electronic Store	
Family income	Less than $20,000	38	54	59	64
		59.4%	84.4%	92.2%	100.0%
	$20,000 to $24,999	32	37	41	43
		74.4%	86.0%	95.3%	100.0%
	$25,000 to $34,999	74	93	101	103
		71.8%	90.3%	98.1%	100.0%
	$35,000 to $44,999	79	92	97	101
		78.2%	91.1%	96.0%	100.0%
	$45,000 to $54,999	37	40	47	49
		75.5%	81.6%	95.9%	100.0%
	$55,000 to $64,999	33	29	36	38
		86.8%	76.3%	94.7%	100.0%
	$65,000 to $74,999	19	26	28	28
		67.9%	92.9%	100.0%	100.0%
	$75,000 or more	34	39	41	47
		72.3%	83.0%	87.2%	100.0%

Complex Tables

The Tables procedure can produce highly complex tables. The next two examples present two types of complex tables commonly used in survey research.

Stacked Table

Thus far, all of the tables we've seen have included only two variables, but Tables can place many variables in either the rows or columns of a table. There is no fixed limit to the size of a table, so as variables are added, the table continues to grow.

One way to add variables to a table is by stacking them, or placing them side by side, in the rows or columns. If we request a table with the shopping multiple response variable in the rows and gender and product type in the columns, Tables generates the output shown in Figure 7.12.

Figure 7.12   A stacked table

Where Shop For Electronic Products?	Male	Female	Product Type	
			Fax Machine	Personal Copier
Shopped in Department Store	167	278	361	84
	75.6%	72.8%	77.3%	61.8%
Shopped in Office Product Store	202	331	413	120
	91.4%	86.6%	88.4%	88.2%
Shopped In Consumer Electronic Store	207	361	437	131
	93.7%	94.5%	93.6%	96.3%
Cases				
	221	382	467	136

In addition to showing the response percentages (within each column) and counts in the cells, the Cases row displays the total number of respondents in each column who answered this question. We've made a few other modifications, both within the Tables procedure and using the Pivot Table Editor, to improve the appearance of this table.

Nested Table

The other common type of table with more than two variables is a nested table. Nesting is a way to combine two or more dimensions into one dimension. To see this in action, we'll take the table in Figure 7.12 and nest product type under gender. The result is shown in Figure 7.13.

Figure 7.13   A nested table

Where Shop For Electronic Products?	Male		Female	
	Fax Machine	Personal Copier	Fax Machine	Personal Copier
Shopped in Department Store	141	26	220	58
	77.5%	66.7%	77.2%	59.8%
Shopped in Office Product Store	165	37	248	83
	90.7%	94.9%	87.0%	85.6%
Shopped In Consumer Electronic Store	171	36	266	95
	94.0%	92.3%	93.3%	97.9%
Cases	182	39	285	97

As you can see, the two categories of product type—fax machine and personal copier—are both displayed under each category of gender. This table is equivalent to a three-variable crosstabulation where gender is the layer variable.

The Tables procedure has many other features, including the ability to calculate summary statistics, such as the mean. It also has many separate formatting options that, combined with the Pivot Table Editor, offer great flexibility in creating exactly the table needed for a report or presentation.

8 Analyzing and Displaying Scales

Surveys are conducted to gather opinions, and the most common method for recording these opinions is with a response scale (such as *Agree/Disagree* or *Satisfied/Dissatisfied*). The analysis of such scales is the focus of this chapter.

As discussed in Chapter 2, it is most proper statistically to consider scales with 5 to 10 response categories as ordinal. Chapter 6 reviewed methods of analyzing and reporting on nominal and ordinal data that are also appropriate for these scales.

At the same time, as we will see in this chapter, scales of five points or more are often treated as interval for many types of analyses by experienced survey researchers. Treating a variable as interval implies that the arithmetic average (the mean) is useful for describing the central tendency of the variable, instead of, or in addition to, the mode (the most common value) and the median (the score at the midpoint of the distribution).

In this chapter, we'll concentrate on summary statistics for single variables for the whole group of respondents. In Chapter 9, we'll review methods for reporting about and testing for group differences in mean scores.

Frequencies

The SPSS Frequencies procedure can calculate a variety of summary statistics. The Frequencies Statistics dialog box is shown in Figure 8.1.

Figure 8.1   Frequencies Statistics dialog box

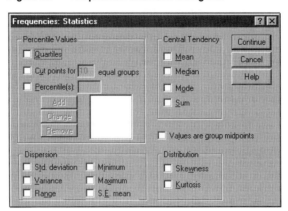

The statistics that can be requested are grouped into categories of Percentile Values, Central Tendency, Dispersion, and Distribution. We'll select Mean and Median in the Central Tendency group, and we'll select the standard deviation (Std. deviation) and the standard error (S.E. mean) in the Dispersion group. In this example, we'll examine the variables *preliabl*, which measures the reliability of the Personal Electronic Products (PEP) product on a 7-point scale, and *satisf_2*, which measures overall satisfaction on a 10-point scale. The statistics used to show characteristics about the distribution—skewness and kurtosis—are not useful for scales.

To make the statistics easier to interpret, make sure that the variables are coded so that higher scores are associated with greater levels of whatever is being measured.

After processing the request, the Output Navigator contains the requested statistics. The table is displayed in Figure 8.2.

Figure 8.2   Summary statistics from Frequencies

Statistics

	N		Mean		Median	Std. Deviation
	Valid	Missing				
	Statistic	Statistic	Statistic	Std. Error	Statistic	Statistic
Performance: Reliability	549	56	6.38	5.50E-02	7.00	1.29
Overall Satisfaction -- 10 Point Scale	600	5	7.93	8.10E-02	8.00	1.98

The mean for reliability is high—6.38 on a seven-point scale. The mean for overall satisfaction is 7.93. Notice that the response at the midpoint of each variable, the median, is close to the mean—7 for reliability and 8 for overall satisfaction. Customers definitely rated PEP products highly on both items, well above the midpoints of each scale.

The standard deviation is a measure of dispersion about the mean. It is equal to the square root of the variance. In comparing one variable to another, standard deviations are most useful when they are measured on the same scale. For example, the standard deviation for satisfaction is 1.98—larger than the 1.29 for reliability—but since satisfaction is measured on a scale with three more possible responses, it will, all things being equal, often have a larger standard deviation.

Descriptives

An alternative to Frequencies, the SPSS Descriptives procedure can quickly produce some of the most important summary statistics. From the menus choose:

Statistics
  Summarize ▶
    Descriptives...

The Descriptives dialog box is shown in Figure 8.3. By default, Descriptives produces the mean, standard deviation, minimum and maximum values, and number of valid responses; however, others can be selected.

Figure 8.3   Descriptives dialog box

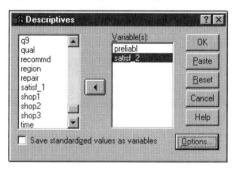

Descriptives allows you to save standardized scores, or Z scores, for one or more variables. These scores are more advantageous when studying interval variables with many categories (age measured in years). The output from Descriptives is shown in Figure 8.4.

Figure 8.4   Descriptives output for reliability and satisfaction ratings

Descriptive Statistics

	Performance: Reliability	Overall Satisfaction -- 10 Point Scale	Valid N (listwise)
N	549	600	544
Minimum	1	1	
Maximum	7	10	
Mean	6.38	7.92	
Std. Deviation	1.29	1.98	

We've used the Pivot Table Editor to transpose the statistics and variables. Some users prefer to use Descriptives to produce these summary statistics because a frequency table is not produced with the statistics. However, there is an option in Frequencies to turn off the table display, so the choice of which procedure to use is one of personal preference. (You should also note that Descriptives does not produce the median.)

Graphical Presentation of Means

Displaying results graphically can be a helpful accompaniment to tabular presentation. Normally, the best choice for presenting the mean for a scale is a bar chart.

Select Bar on the Graph menu to open the Bar Charts dialog box, as shown in Figure 8.5.

Figure 8.5   Bar Charts dialog box

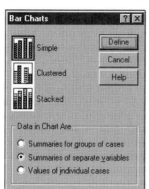

Since we want to display the mean of a variable, select Summaries of separate variables under Data in Chart Are.

Next, click Define to open the Summaries of Separate Variables dialog box, as shown in Figure 8.6, and specify the variables on which to report.

Figure 8.6   Summaries of Separate Variables dialog box

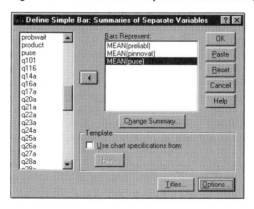

We'll display the mean score for *preliabl*, *pinnovat*, and *puse* (reliability, innovation, and ease of use). You can use the Options pushbutton to change the treatment of missing data. By default, cases are not used to calculate the mean if they are missing for any of the variables. You may want to change this to exclude missing data on a variable-by-variable basis.

Click OK to display the bar chart in the Output Navigator, as shown in Figure 8.7. It is important when using this type of graph that all of the variables be measured on the same scale. If one scale has 10 points and another has 7 points, or if different labels are used for the endpoints, you will be comparing apples and oranges.

Figure 8.7   Bar chart displaying means for preliabl, pinnovat, and puse

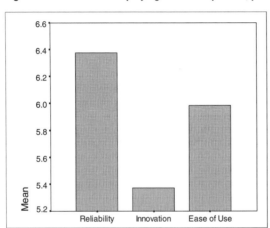

Reliability has the highest mean at about 6.4. Ease of use is next with about 6.0, and innovation is lowest at about 5.4. These differences tend to be exaggerated by the scale used on the vertical axis, which runs only from 5.0 to 6.6, even though these variables are measured on a scale that runs from 1 to 7. Sometimes it is better to change the vertical axis to make the range of the variables explicit, which we did in Figure 8.8 (using the Chart Editor feature).

Figure 8.8   Modified bar chart displaying means

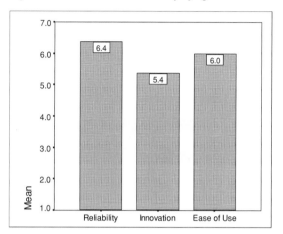

In addition to modifying the scale axis, we also added the mean value to each bar to make it easier to read the chart. It is now obvious that the means, while different, are all above the midpoint value of 4 for the scale range, and the differences between the means are not as exaggerated. Neither chart is necessarily more correct than the other. However, the second chart shows the importance of modifying the default format when it does not correspond to the requirements of your specific application.

Explore

You can use the SPSS Explore procedure to calculate descriptive statistics, as you've done with Frequencies and Descriptives, and to generate plots that show how a variable is distributed. In particular, Explore calculates a **confidence interval** for a variable, which is a set of upper and lower bounds that bracket the likely values for a parameter being estimated from a survey (in our case, the mean for the variables).

To run the SPSS Explore procedure, from the menus choose:

Statistics
  Summarize ▶
    Explore...

This opens the Explore dialog box, as shown in Figure 8.9. By default, Explore produces statistics and two types of graphs.

Figure 8.9   Explore dialog box

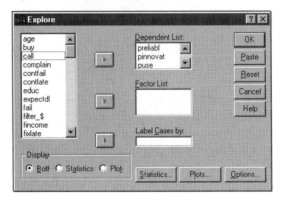

Click **Plots** to open the Explore Plots dialog box and select **Dependents together** in the Boxplots group. This selection will ensure that Explore displays one chart with all three variables rather than a separate chart for each variable.

The statistics produced by Explore are shown in Figure 8.10 (this table was modified in the Pivot Table Editor). The statistics produced by Frequencies and Descriptives are also included in the table, as are several others. We will focus on the confidence interval.

To review the concept of sampling error and confidence intervals, see Chapter 3.

You know that the estimates of the mean rating for reliability, innovation, and ease of use from this sample are unlikely to be equal to the population value for all of PEP's customers. A confidence interval takes into account sampling variability to provide an estimate of the likely error in estimates of the mean. The 95% confidence interval is calculated so that 95 times out of 100, the interval you calculate should include the population value. It is calculated using the standard error of the mean (also shown in Figure 8.10). Equation 8.1 shows the formula for the 95% confidence interval for a mean:

$$\overline{X} \pm 1.96\sigma_{\overline{X}}$$

Equation 8.1

The confidence interval is simply the mean value ($\overline{X}$), plus or minus an estimate of sampling error. The standard error of the mean ($\sigma_{\overline{X}}$)—which is the standard deviation of the distribution of sample means—is multiplied by a scaling factor based on the normal curve. For the 95% confidence interval, this value is 1.96. The 95% confidence interval is the most common, but SPSS can calculate intervals for any confidence level. Other typical choices are the 90% and 99% level.

Figure 8.10   Summary statistics produced by Explore

Descriptives

			Performance: Reliability	Performance: Innovative Company	Performance: Ease of Use
	Mean		6.37	5.37	5.98
	95% Confidence Interval for Mean	Lower Bound	6.26	5.22	5.87
		Upper Bound	6.48	5.52	6.10
	5% Trimmed Mean		6.60	5.50	6.16
	Median		7.00	6.00	6.00
	Variance		1.591	2.920	1.812
	Std. Deviation		1.26	1.71	1.35
	Minimum		1	1	1
	Maximum		7	7	7
	Range		6	6	6
	Interquartile Range		1.00	2.00	1.00
	Skewness		-2.973	-.983	-1.870
	Kurtosis		8.948	-.098	3.430
Std. Error	Mean		5.58E-02	7.56E-02	5.95E-02
	Skewness		.108	.108	.108
	Kurtosis		.216	.216	.216

The 95% confidence interval for innovation ranges from 5.22 to 5.52. Its correct interpretation is that 95 times out of 100, for sample sizes of 511 (the number of valid responses using listwise deletion), the confidence interval calculated for innovation will include the unknown population value. For this *particular* sample, the confidence interval either does or does not include the population value, so you should avoid saying something like *There's a 95% probability that the population mean ranges from 5.22 to 5.52*. Instead, state that *There's a 95% probability that the confidence interval includes the population mean*.

Nevertheless, the confidence interval remains the best estimate of the mean. In other words, you estimate that customers rate PEP's innovation from 5.22 to 5.52 on a seven-point scale. This is a reasonably narrow interval, and the 95%

confidence intervals for reliability and ease of use are even narrower. You can see why if you examine the standard errors for each variable. Being able to place a confidence interval on the mean for a scale is enormously helpful because it makes you aware of the error inherent in sample estimates.

Boxplots

Explore produces a chart called a boxplot that displays the median, spread, and minimum and maximum values for a variable. Boxplots are useful for displaying the distribution of interval or ratio variables, and they can be even more helpful when used with interval variables that have many categories, such as age.

Figure 8.11 shows the boxplot for the three variables we've been exploring. The solid black line is the median; the gray rectangle extends from the 25th to the 75th percentile (that is, the middle 50% of the distribution); and the whiskers extend to the largest and smallest observed values within 1½ times the height of each rectangle. If there are any points outside the whiskers, they are labeled with case ID's (difficult to read here because several customers gave the same response) and generally called outliers.

Figure 8.11   Boxplot for reliability, innovation, and ease-of-use ratings

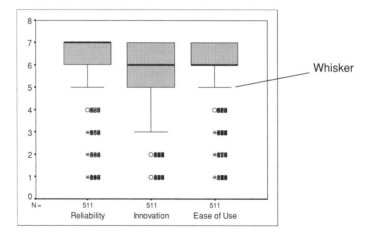

In this plot, you can see the greater variability, or spread, of the innovation rating, since it has a longer rectangle than reliability and ease of use. This greater spread leads to its larger confidence interval. Notice also that the upper end of each rectangle reaches the upper limit of the scale range (7). This is because the ratings are very high, so the 75th percentile is at the upper end of the scale.

Error Bar Charts

Another chart type that can be used to display the confidence interval for one or more variables is the error bar chart. It can be used to supplement the tabular information in Figure 8.10. To create this type of chart, choose Error Bar from the Graphs menu. As you did for the standard bar charts in Figure 8.7 and Figure 8.8, select Summaries of separate variables in the Error Bar dialog box. Click Define to open the Define Simple Error Bar dialog box, as shown in Figure 8.12.

Figure 8.12   Define Simple Error Bar dialog box

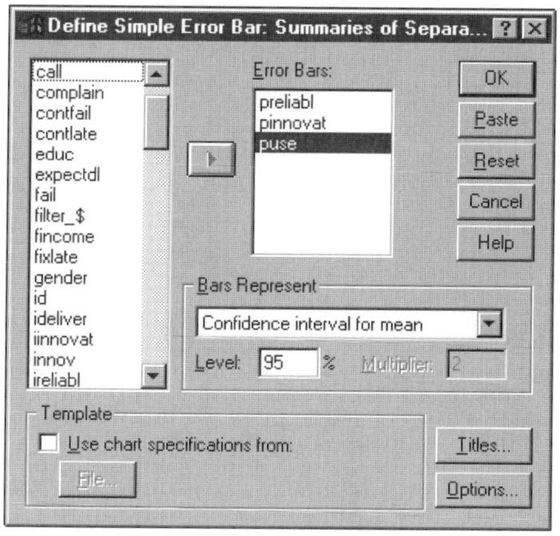

By default, the bars produced by SPSS will represent the 95% confidence interval. (You can change this by typing a different value in the Level text box.) The error bar chart produced from this request is shown in Figure 8.13.

Figure 8.13   95% confidence intervals for three performance variables

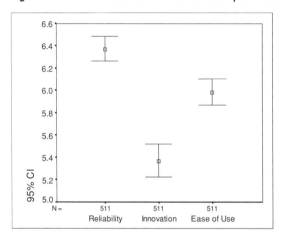

The height of each bar represents the confidence interval. The small square designates the mean. Compare this chart to Figure 8.7. You'll see that error bar charts can be a handy way to display sampling error for those who prefer to get information visually.

Testing a Single Mean

In this chapter, we have examined summary statistics and graphical displays of those statistics for scales. We have not compared one mean to another to see whether the rating for reliability is greater than that for ease of use. We will investigate methods to formally answer this question in Chapter 9.

There are many occasions in survey research, however, when you want to compare the mean for one variable to its value in another sample. For example, you can compare the results from last year's rating of reliability to the results from this year's sample to find out whether the respondents think you're now doing better (or worse). A statistical test can be made to determine whether there has been any shift in rating from one year to the next, but choosing the correct test requires some care.

The SPSS One-Sample T Test procedure compares the mean of a variable to a test value. Many people believe that this is the most appropriate method for comparing the current rating of reliability to the value of the mean from a previous survey. The fundamental error in this approach is that the one-sample *t* test considers the test value as a fixed number *with no error*. This is not true for the rating from last year because that rating was a sample estimate, with all its attendant error.

The most direct method for comparing the means of the same variables from two surveys is to merge the two data sets together and then conduct a standard *t* test for a mean difference. That's easy to do if you've kept a copy of last year's file. If you haven't, you'll still have to know the standard deviation, number of responses, and mean from the last sample to run the test.

SPSS can help you do the test, although it may be just as easy to use a calculator. The *SPSS Guide to Data Analysis* contains the necessary formula in the section on testing a hypothesis about two independent means.

One-Sample T Test

So, under what circumstances would you want to use the One-Sample T Test procedure? Consider this situation. You know from U. S. census figures that the mean number of years of education for all adults is 13.6. You'd like to know whether PEP customers have more or less education than the adult population. The One-Sample T Test procedure will compare the test value of 13.6 to the PEP customers' mean education, using the same information used to construct the confidence interval, to determine the probability that the sample value is no different from the population value. (We used a one-sample chi-square test in Chapter 5 to test for response bias for the categorical variable *product*, and a one-sample *t* test can be used in the same way with interval data.)

Another, possibly more likely, situation in which you would use this test is to compare a sample mean to a preset performance value. Let's say that PEP management set a goal of having the ease-of-use customer rating attain a mean of 6 on the seven-point scale because they believe that ease of use is a critical factor in satisfaction. The actual sample mean was 5.91, which obviously differs from 6 (no bonuses this year). Still, the sample mean is subject to sampling error, and a value of 5.91 may be compatible with a true population value of 6.

To run this procedure, from the menus choose:

Statistics
  Compare Means ▶
    One-Sample T Test...

This opens the One-Sample T Test dialog box, as shown in Figure 8.14.

Figure 8.14   One-Sample T Test dialog box

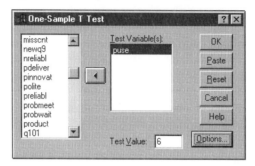

The test will be done at the 95% confidence level by default (you can change the level by clicking Options). We've moved the test variable *puse* into the list and specified a test value of 6.

Figure 8.15 shows the output from the test. The first table presents the familiar summary statistics for *puse*. The second table presents the actual test.

Figure 8.15   One-Sample T Test for ease of use (test value of 6)

One-Sample Statistics

	N	Mean	Std. Deviation	Std. Error Mean
Ease of Use	565	5.91	1.39	5.85E-02

One-Sample Test

	Test Value = 6					
					95% Confidence Interval of the Difference	
	t	df	Sig. (2-tailed)	Mean Difference	Lower	Upper
Ease of Use	-1.542	564	.124	-9.03E-02	-.21	2.47E-02

The *t* distribution is used in this test. The calculated *t* value −1.542 (negative because the test value is greater than the sample value) is used, with the degrees of freedom, to calculate a significance level, labeled *Sig. (2-tailed)*. The significance level, which you have encountered in Chapter 6, tells you how likely you are to find a mean difference between the sample and the population as great as, or greater than, 0.09. In this case, it might happen about 12 times out of 100 samples, since the significance is 0.124.

If this probability appears likely enough, you might successfully argue that the sample mean of 5.91 for the ease-of-use rating shouldn't preclude a bonus for everyone, since statistically speaking, you can't distinguish this value from 6.0.

This concludes our examination of how to summarize and report on scale variables. In Chapter 9, we'll look at the most common SPSS procedures used to test for group differences and to develop models for prediction.

9 Quantitative Analysis

Most survey researchers are not satisfied with simply reporting what the respondents, as a whole, think about whatever issues were raised on the questionnaire. Rather, a common goal is to determine whether there are differences between groups of respondents; a second goal is to develop models to help predict attitude or behavior.

SPSS contains many powerful procedures that can accomplish these goals for variables that are measured on interval or ratio scales. This chapter discusses several of the more commonly used procedures. All of the procedures discussed are included in the SPSS Base system.

Differences in Means

The Personal Electronic Products (PEP) survey contained a question asking whether PEP products were a good value for the money. PEP has been wondering whether customers who own fax machines gave higher ratings on this question than those who own personal copiers. Additionally, PEP suspects that there are differences in attitude depending on family income level.

When you begin to search for potential group differences, rather than first calculating a statistical test, begin by using an SPSS procedure to display the group means for the variables of interest. The Means procedure is a good choice.

To run the Means procedure, from the menus choose:

Statistics
  Compare Means ▶
    Means...

This opens the Means dialog box, as shown in Figure 9.1. For this example, we've moved *value* to the Dependent List and *product* and *fincome* to the Independent List. The default statistics are the mean, the number of cases, and the standard deviation. (Clicking Options would let you choose additional statistics.)

Figure 9.1   Means dialog box

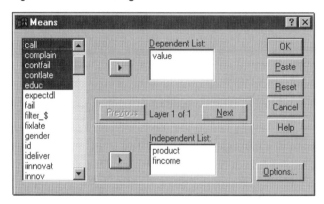

After you click OK, SPSS runs the request. Figure 9.2 shows the output for product type. *Value* is measured on a seven-point scale, from *Strongly disagree* to *Strongly agree*, and both owners of fax machines and personal copiers have a relatively high mean score. Moreover, the difference between the two means is only 0.05 scale points, which is inconsequential. When a difference between two or more means is obviously not substantively significant (of importance in the real world), you don't need to do any statistical testing. Even if there is a statistically significant difference, when it's not large enough to make a consequential difference, the test results are irrelevant.

Figure 9.2   Summary statistics for value by product type

Performance: Good value for money

		Mean	N	Std. Deviation
Product Type	Fax Machine	5.95	464	1.43
	Personal Copier	6.00	136	1.33
	Total	5.96	600	1.41

Figure 9.3 shows the output for family income. (The table has been modified by using the Pivot Table Editor to increase the width of the *Family income* column.)

Figure 9.3   Summary statistics for value by family income

Performance: Good value for money

		Mean	N	Std. Deviation
Family income	Less than $20,000	5.89	64	1.33
	$20,000 to $24,999	6.60	43	.49
	$25,000 to $34,999	6.39	103	.95
	$35,000 to $44,999	6.44	101	.94
	$45,000 to $54,999	5.92	48	1.32
	$55,000 to $64,999	6.14	36	1.36
	$65,000 to $74,999	4.64	28	1.62
	$75,000 or more	4.79	47	1.89
	Total	6.02	470	1.35

You can use other techniques besides Means to examine relationships in your data. For example, use Crosstabs to look at value by family income, since both variables have a small number of categories.

Unlike the results for product type, the results for family income show differences. The overall mean is high, although not identical to that in the table for product type (because fewer respondents answered the income question). But except for the lowest income category, there seems to be a pattern of lower means at higher income levels. This is especially true for those earning $65,000 or more. The mean rating for these two groups is probably low enough to cause PEP some concern.

When you review tables produced by the Means procedure, you should also look in the column labeled *N* to see how many responses were recorded in each category of the independent variable. If the number of cases is low—perhaps fewer than 20—you'll need to consider taking the following actions:

- Use the Recode procedure to combine the category with fewer responses with an adjacent category.

- Exclude this group from any tests because of the small sample size.

- Be extremely careful in interpreting results for this category.

Later in the chapter, we'll use the One-Way ANOVA procedure to see if the mean differences shown in Figure 9.3 are statistically significant.

Displaying Group Differences Graphically

We used the Explore procedure in Chapter 8 to look at the distribution of scale variables. This procedure can also display boxplots for separate groups of respondents to further explore mean differences before doing statistical testing. The Explore dialog box is shown in Figure 9.4.

Figure 9.4   Explore dialog box

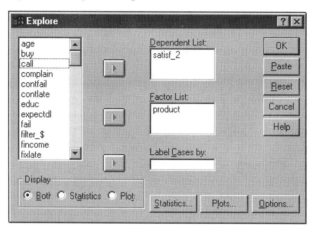

In this example, the variable *satisf_2* (measuring satisfaction on a 10-point scale) is the dependent variable, and *product* (product type) is the factor, or independent variable. Recall from Figure 9.2 that the type of product a customer owns doesn't affect his or her rating of whether PEP products are good values for the money, but perhaps there is a difference for overall satisfaction.

Figure 9.5 shows the output for overall satisfaction. (This table has been modified using the Pivot Table Editor to delete some unnecessary statistics and labels and to transpose rows and columns.)

Figure 9.5   Summary statistics for overall satisfaction by product type

Descriptives

			Overall Satisfaction -- 10 Point Scale	
			Product Type	
			Fax Machine	Personal Copier
Statistic	Mean		7.88	8.10
	95% Confidence Interval for Mean	Lower Bound	7.70	7.74
		Upper Bound	8.05	8.46
	Median		8.00	9.00
	Variance		3.787	4.452
	Std. Deviation		1.95	2.11
	Interquartile Range		2.00	3.00
	Skewness		-1.193	-1.373
	Kurtosis		1.380	1.700

The mean satisfaction rating for owners of fax machines is 7.88; that for owners of personal copiers is 8.1. This difference is still not large, and both groups of customers give a reasonably high rating to overall satisfaction. The 95% confidence interval is listed for both groups, and that for personal copier owners is much wider (approximately 0.7 of a scale point) than that for fax machine owners (0.35). Although the standard deviations for the two groups are roughly comparable, the wider confidence interval for personal copier owners is due to the smaller number of respondents in this group. There are 467 fax machine owners and 133 personal copier owners. (This information was included in the first table produced by Explore, which is not shown here.)

Figure 9.6 shows the boxplot for overall satisfaction.

Figure 9.6   Boxplot for overall satisfaction by product type

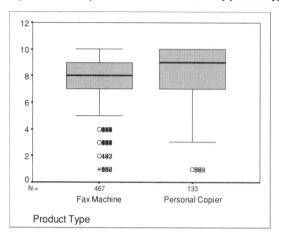

The greater variability of responses by personal copier owners is represented by the greater height of their rectangle. The rectangle height is the interquartile range, and Figure 9.5 shows that the value for personal copier owners is 3, while the value for fax machine owners is 2.

The spread for personal copier owners is great enough so that the only out-lying cases are those who rated overall satisfaction as a 1. The distribution for fax machine owners is more compact, so outlying cases here include ratings of 1, 2, 3, and 4. More than one customer gave these responses, so the case ID's that SPSS prints are hard to read (the Chart Editor supplies a Point Identification tool that allows you to see a list of all cases at each response).

Now that you've reviewed the group differences, you're ready to use SPSS to calculate statistical tests. In the following section, you'll begin by seeing whether the overall satisfaction ratings do differ by product type.

Independent-Samples T Test

The Independent-Samples T Test procedure tests whether two population means are equal based on the results from two independent samples. It may seem odd to think of fax machine and personal copier owners as coming from two independent samples, but they do. When PEP selected its sample of cus-tomers, the selection of a particular fax machine owner had nothing to do with the selection of a personal copier owner. In other words, there is no relationship between the two groups.

The Independent-Samples T Test procedure is accessed from Compare Means on the Statistics menu. Figure 9.7 shows the Independent-Samples T Test dialog box.

Figure 9.7   Independent-Samples T Test dialog box

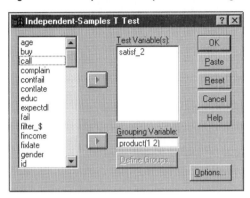

Product is the grouping, or independent, variable. (Notice that SPSS requires the codes for the two categories of product type, specified in the Define Groups dialog box, which is not shown here.) The options available include the specification of the confidence level to use. Although SPSS provides an exact significance level, when calculating a confidence interval for the mean difference between the two groups, it uses the 95% level by default. The null hypothesis for the test is that the two groups have equal means for overall satisfaction.

Figure 9.8 shows the output for the independent-samples *t* test. There are two sets of results, one labeled *Equal variances assumed* and the other, *Equal variances not assumed*.

Figure 9.8   Independent-samples t test output

Independent Samples Test

		Levene's Test for Equality of Variances		t-test for Equality of Means						
									95% Confidence Interval of the Mean	
		F	Sig.	t	df	Sig. (2-tailed)	Mean Difference	Std. Error Difference	Lower	Upper
Overall Satisfaction -- 10 Point Scale	Equal variances assumed	1.532	.216	-1.138	598	.255	-.22	.19	-.60	.16
	Equal variances not assumed			-1.088	200.366	.278	-.22	.20	-.62	.18

T Test Assumptions

All statistical tests make assumptions about the data. As tests become more powerful and complex, they generally make more assumptions. In Chapter 7, you saw that the chi-square test for crosstabulation assumed, or required, that the expected count in each cell of a table was at least five.

The independent-samples t test assumes that the data are normally distributed with the same population variance for both groups. The normality assumption is not too critical for large sample sizes, but the equality of variance assumption must always be tested. Fortunately, there is a formula available for an independent-samples t test that can adjust for unequal variances, but first you must test the variances.

This test is called the **Levene Test**. Its null hypothesis is that the variances are equal, and the significance level for the test is 0.216. This is fairly high, so you cannot reject the null hypothesis of equal variance. It is true that the box-plot shown in Figure 9.6 made the dispersion of satisfaction for personal copier owners seem greater, but the variances shown in Figure 9.5 are not that different. This means that you should use the *Equal variances assumed* output. If the Levene test indicated unequal variances, you would use the output in the lower half of the table instead.

Testing for Satisfaction Difference

The t test output has a significance level of 0.255, which means that you have a one-in-four chance of finding a mean difference for overall satisfaction of 0.22 or greater between the two groups of customers if there is no difference in the population. This is reasonably probable, so you can't reject the null hypothesis of no difference.

SPSS also provides a 95% confidence level for the difference, which ranges from –0.60 to 0.16. The fact that it includes the value 0 is another indication that you can't reject the null hypothesis. The sample results are compatible with not only the null hypothesis, however. It is also possible that the mean satisfaction level for fax machine owners is 0.60 points lower than that for personal copier owners (the –0.60 lower bound), or that the mean satisfaction level for the former group is 0.16 points *higher* than that for the latter group (the 0.16 upper bound).

Paired-Samples T Test

Survey researchers are typically interested in comparing the means of two variables to see if respondents gave a higher rating to one or the other. The variables often record product or service attribute ratings. For example, account holders might rate the teller and electronic banking services at a bank, and the bank management would like to know whether one or the other was rated more favorably. To answer this type of question, use the Paired-Samples T Test procedure.

Remember that the two variables must be measured on the same scale. You can't compare a 5-point to a 10-point scale.

This test is different from the independent-samples *t* test because instead of comparing the mean of one variable for two groups, it compares the mean of two variables for one group. Specifically, each respondent has provided an answer for both variables, which violates the common assumption in statistical testing of independence between observations.

For this example, recall Chapter 8, specifically Figure 8.8, where the ratings of three variables concerning the performance of PEP products were compared. Let's conduct a test to see if the mean rating for reliability is different from that for ease of use.

Figure 9.9 shows the Paired-Samples T Test dialog box. When you click on one variable (here *preliabl*), it is moved into the Current Selections list. When you click on a second variable, it is also moved into the list, so that the variables are paired to SPSS. You then move the pair into the Paired Variables list.

Figure 9.9   Paired-Samples T Test dialog box

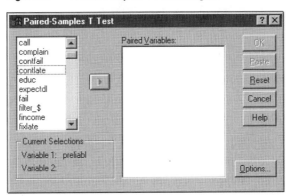

Figure 9.10 shows the output (in three separate tables) for the paired-samples *t* test.

Figure 9.10   Paired-samples t test output

Paired Samples Statistics

		Mean	N	Std. Deviation	Std. Error Mean
Pair 1	Reliability	6.37	511	1.26	5.58E-02
	Ease of Use	5.98	511	1.35	5.95E-02

Paired Samples Correlations

		N	Correlation	Sig.
Pair 1	Reliability & Ease of Use	511	.273	.000

Paired Samples Test

		Paired Differences							
					95% Confidence Interval of the Difference				
		Mean	Std. Deviation	Std. Error Mean	Lower	Upper	t	df	Sig. (2-tailed)
Pair 1	Reliability - Ease of Use	.39	1.57	6.96E-02	.25	.53	5.593	510	.000

Note that the significance level is two-tailed. This test is looking for any difference in the reliability and ease-of-use ratings. To detect a predicted difference in only one direction (such as which variable would have a higher rating), use a one-tailed test. For a one-tailed test, the significance level is divided by 2.

SPSS first displays summary statistics. As a reminder, you see that the mean for reliability (on a seven-point scale) is 6.37, and the mean for ease of use is 5.98. (Note that the standard error of the mean is displayed using scientific notation. In previous examples in this and other chapters, we have changed the format by using the Pivot Table Editor.) The sample size for this test is 511 because 511 customers answered both questions.

The second table shows the correlation coefficient between the two variables. The higher the value—that is, the closer to 1—the more power you have to detect a significant difference. However, power is also related to sample size, which is reasonably large in this instance (you'll learn more about correlation beginning on p. 140).

The third table contains the actual test results. The paired-samples *t* test doesn't have an assumption of equal variances, so there is only one *t* test. The significance level is listed in the far right column. Its value is small, less than 0.0005 (the value is rounded). Using the Pivot Table Editor, you can reformat the cell to discover the exact significance level, which turns out to be 0.000000036. This value is so small and so far below any normal criterion level of 0.05 or 0.01 that you can be secure in rejecting the null hypothesis of no difference in ratings for reliability and ease of use. Specifically, the rating for reliability is higher than that for ease of use.

As with the independent-samples *t* test, a 95% confidence interval is supplied for the mean difference. It ranges from 0.25 to 0.53, a fairly narrow interval. It's now up to the management at PEP to decide whether the statistically significant difference in rating for these two characteristics is of substantive importance.

Testing Differences for More Than Two Groups

When you have more than two groups to compare, the *t* test is not adequate. You should instead use a variety of techniques known as analysis of variance (ANOVA). In Figure 9.3, you looked at differences in the mean ratings for value by family income. A pattern, which indicated that those with higher incomes appeared to think that PEP products were not such a good value for the money, emerged. To test this, you would use the SPSS One-Way ANOVA procedure.

One-Way Analysis of Variance

The One-Way ANOVA procedure is the simplest procedure in SPSS to test for mean differences for more than two groups.

To run this procedure, from the menus choose:

Statistics
  Compare Means ▶
    One-Way ANOVA...

Figure 9.11 (on the left) shows the One-Way ANOVA dialog box. The Dependent and Factor lists show the dependent and independent variables, respectively. Unlike the independent-samples *t* test, the range of the independent variable does not need to be specified.

Figure 9.11   One-Way ANOVA and Post Hoc dialog boxes

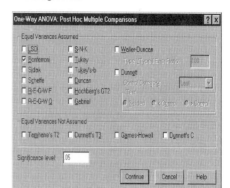

Figure 9.11 (on the right) shows the Post Hoc Multiple Comparisons dialog box. Whenever you use the One-Way ANOVA procedure, you'll need to specify at least one post hoc multiple comparison test.

The interpretation of the result of a *t* test is clear: if there is a statistically significant mean difference, which mean is higher and which mean is lower is obvious. This is not the case when more than two groups are compared. A statistically significant test tells you only that it is unlikely that all of the group means in the population are different, but not which groups are different from each other. The multiple comparison tests will give us this information.

The assumption of equal group variances also applies here. The Levene test can be calculated by SPSS to see if the assumption is violated.

For this example, we've selected the Bonferroni multiple comparison test. (A complete discussion of the multiple comparison tests is beyond the scope of this text.)

Figure 9.12 shows the one-way ANOVA output for value by family income. The significance value is small, 0.000 (less than 0.0005), which means that you can reject the null hypothesis of no difference in the rating of good value for the money by income level. (The remainder of the statistics in the table can be ignored, but they were all used to calculate the significance level.)

Figure 9.12   One-Way ANOVA output for value by family income

ANOVA

		Sum of Squares	df	Mean Square	F	Sig.
Performance: Good value for money	Between Groups	172.743	7	24.678	16.666	.000
	Within Groups	684.084	462	1.481		
	Total	856.828	469			

The next step is to examine the output from the multiple comparison test, which is shown in Figure 9.13 (only the first panel of the table is displayed).

Figure 9.13   Bonferroni multiple comparison test

Multiple Comparisons

Dependent Variable: Performance: Good value for money

Bonferroni

(I) Family income	(J) Family income	Mean Difference (I-J)	Std. Error	Sig.	95% Confidence Interval Lower Bound	95% Confidence Interval Upper Bound
Less than $20,000	$20,000 to $24,999	-.71	.240	.086	-1.47	3.99E-02
	$25,000 to $34,999	-.50	.194	.294	-1.11	.11
	$35,000 to $44,999	-.55	.194	.148	-1.16	6.58E-02
	$45,000 to $54,999	-2.60E-02	.232	1.000	-.76	.70
	$55,000 to $64,999	-.25	.254	1.000	-1.04	.55
	$65,000 to $74,999	1.25*	.276	.000	.38	2.11
	$75,000 or more	1.10*	.234	.000	.37	1.84

The table is divided into eight panels, one for each income category. Within each panel, the test compares the mean of *value* for the reference income level to all of the other levels of income. For example, the difference in mean between those earning less than $20,000 and those earning from $20,000 to $24,999 is –0.71 (the negative sign indicates that the reference category— $20,000—is lower). This difference is not significant at the 0.05 level, as you can see in the *Sig.* column.

As you review the output, recall Figure 9.3, where the mean for each income category is listed. The mean rating for the value of PEP products by those earning less than $20,000 is significantly higher than that for the two highest income categories, but not different from the other categories. This confirms what we noticed informally before.

A multiple comparison test pinpoints why the overall analysis-of-variance test was significant. It appears that PEP has indeed discovered that those earning $65,000 and more think that PEP products are not as good a value for the money.

Correlation and Linear Regression

When you study the relationship between two or more variables measured on at least an ordinal scale (and more appropriately, an interval or ratio scale), you can use the techniques of correlation and linear regression. For example, how is age related to overall satisfaction? Do individual product and service attributes help to predict overall satisfaction? Both of these questions are concerned with the *association* between two or more variables, rather than comparing the mean of one variable within categories of another.

The PEP company is interested in seeing what factors predict overall satisfaction. (We'll use the variable *satisf_2*, measured on a 10-point scale, for the best approximation of interval-scaled data.) PEP will try to predict satisfaction with three items: age, income, and the reliability rating of PEP products.

Correlation

Before using the Regression procedure to see which, if any, of these variables is a good predictor, you should do some initial examination of the data. For regression analysis, one of the first steps is to look at the association between each pair of variables. You can use the SPSS Correlations procedure.

To run this procedure, from the menus choose:

Statistics
  Correlate ▶
    Bivariate...

This opens the Bivariate Correlations dialog box, as shown in Figure 9.14. The variables for overall satisfaction, age, income, and reliability rating have been moved into the Variables list. By default, the Pearson correlation coefficient is calculated. (For data you want to consider as ordinal, the Spearman correlation coefficient is available.)

Figure 9.14   Bivariate Correlations dialog box

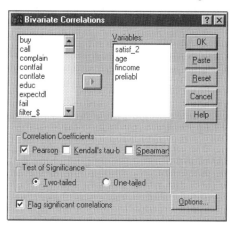

Figure 9.15 shows the Correlations procedure output.

Figure 9.15   Correlations output

Correlations

		Overall Satisfaction -- 10 Point Scale	Age of respondent	Family income	Performance: Reliability
Pearson Correlation	Overall Satisfaction -- 10 Point Scale	1.000	.038	-.370**	.386**
	Age of respondent	.038	1.000	-.008	.046
	Family income	-.370**	-.008	1.000	-.167**
	Performance: Reliability	.386**	.046	-.167**	1.000
Sig. (2-tailed)	Overall Satisfaction -- 10 Point Scale	.	.353	.000	.000
	Age of respondent	.353	.	.855	.278
	Family income	.000	.855	.	.001
	Performance: Reliability	.000	.278	.001	.
N	Overall Satisfaction -- 10 Point Scale	600	598	473	544
	Age of respondent	598	603	475	547
	Family income	473	475	475	431
	Performance: Reliability	544	547	431	549

**. Correlation is significant at the 0.01 level (2-tailed).

The Pearson correlation coefficient is a measure of association for interval or ratio data, just as Somers' d and Kendall's tau are measures of association for ordinal data.

The first panel in the table contains the **Pearson correlation coefficient**. This statistic measures how strongly two variables are related. It ranges in value from +1 to –1. Both large positive and negative values indicate a strong relationship between two variables, but a negative value indicates that higher values of one variable are associated with lower values of the other variable. To graphically display the joint distribution of two intervally scaled variables, use a scatterplot.

The output is symmetric in each panel, so you need to look only at the lower-left or upper-right triangles. The values of 1.000 on the diagonal of the matrix are the correlation of each variable with itself (a perfect correlation). In the *Overall Satisfaction* column, you see that its correlation with age is 0.038; with family income, –0.370; and with reliability, 0.386. The double asterisks indicate that the correlation is significant at the 0.01 level. The null hypothesis is that the correlation in the population is 0. A correlation of 0 appears to be unlikely for income and reliability rating, but you can't reject the null hypothesis for age.

The table also contains the correlations between the variables you'll use as predictors. All of the correlations are low; the highest (in absolute value) is the –0.167 between reliability rating and income.

The actual significance levels for each coefficient are presented in the second panel of the table. Here you see that the correlation between age and satisfaction has a significance level of 0.353. The third panel shows the number of responses used to calculate each correlation coefficient. As always, it is important to notice whether there are a lot of missing data.

It appears that there are two possible predictors of overall satisfaction and one variable that won't be very helpful. The next step is to build a model using all three variables simultaneously to predict satisfaction. Based on the output, you might use only income and reliability rating, since age had essentially a zero correlation coefficient. For this example, however, you'll use all three.

Linear Regression

Regression is a powerful technique that uses one or more predictor variables to explain an outcome, or dependent variable. The data are fit with a straight-line relationship, and the coefficients calculated for each variable measure the effect of one variable *controlling* for the others in the equation. This means that you can measure the unique effect of each predictor on the dependent variable. Looking at correlations between the predictors and the dependent variable is not sufficient to accomplish this because correlations between the *predictors* can confuse the matter. For example, you might find that people with higher incomes (the dependent variable) have more education and live in the suburbs (the two independent variables). However, after you calculate a regression equation, you may learn that the effect of place of residence on income is reduced considerably because the true relationship is between education and income.

Figure 9.16 shows the Linear Regression dialog box. *Satisf_2* is the dependent variable, and *age*, *fincome*, and *preliabl* are the independent variables. (This dialog box has several pushbuttons available to request additional statistics and plots, to save various portions of the output as new variables, and to control the handling of missing data. Regression is too complex a topic to do more than introduce it here, so we encourage you to read more about it in the *SPSS Base User's Guide*.)

Figure 9.16   Linear Regression dialog box

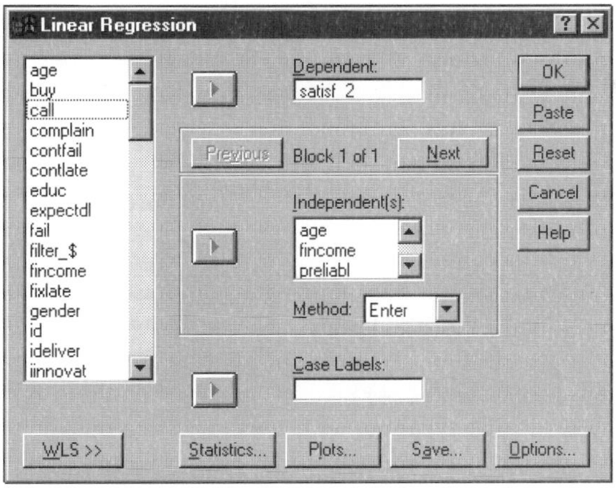

After running the procedure, SPSS produces the output shown in Figure 9.17. (The tables have been slightly modified for display by using the Pivot Table Editor.)

Figure 9.17   Regression of overall satisfaction on age, income, and reliability

Model Summary[1,2]

		Variables		R	R Square	Adjusted R Square	Std. Error of the Estimate
		Entered	Removed				
Model	1	Performance: Reliability, Age of respondent, Family income[3,4]		.	.404	.163	.157	1.69

1. Dependent Variable: Overall Satisfaction -- 10 Point Scale
2. Method: Enter
3. Independent Variables: (Constant), Performance: Reliability, Age of respondent, Family income
4. All requested variables entered.

ANOVA[1]

			Sum of Squares	df	Mean Square	F	Sig.
Model	1	Regression	236.754	3	78.918	27.648	.000[2]
		Residual	1213.097	425	2.854		
		Total	1449.851	428			

1. Dependent Variable: Overall Satisfaction -- 10 Point Scale
2. Independent Variables: (Constant), Performance: Reliability, Age of respondent, Family income

Coefficients[1]

			Unstandardized Coefficients		Standardized Coefficients	t	Sig.
			B	Std. Error	Beta		
Model	1	(Constant)	6.364	.520		12.245	.000
		Age of respondent	3.0E-02	.066	.020	.452	.652
		Family income	-.244	.041	-.271	-6.018	.000
		Performance: Reliability	.392	.069	.256	5.646	.000

1. Dependent Variable: Overall Satisfaction -- 10 Point Scale

The table labeled *Model Summary* contains the *Adjusted R Square* statistic, which measures the amount of variance in overall satisfaction explained by the three independent variables. The adjusted R^2 is 0.157, so 15.7% of the variance in overall satisfaction is explained by the regression equation. This is quite modest and would not be adequate for practical use (but you will undoubtedly include more than three variables in a regression).

The table labeled *ANOVA* contains the statistical test that tells you whether these three variables are significant predictors of satisfaction. The significance value (labeled *Sig.*) is 0.000, so you can conclude that the variables jointly have some predictive power (that is, the R^2 value is not equal to 0).

The table labeled *Coefficients* contains the estimates for the regression equation. The column labeled *Unstandardized Coefficients* (*B*) contains the estimates for the variables in their original scale of measurement. The significance level of each coefficient is listed in the rightmost column. The effect of age remains insignificant, consistent with the bivariate correlation between age and satisfaction. The two other variables' significance levels are low (0.000), so you can conclude that family income and reliability rating are statistically significant predictors of overall satisfaction.

The unstandardized coefficient for income is a negative number, which means that as income increases, satisfaction decreases. Recall that the same type of relationship existed for income and the question about whether PEP products are a good value for the money. The coefficient for reliability rating is a positive number; not surprisingly, people who think their product is more reliable are more satisfied. The actual effect is given by the coefficient, 0.392. Its interpretation is that, controlling for age and income, a one-unit increase in reliability rating (recall that it is measured on a seven-point scale) leads to a 0.392 increase in the overall satisfaction rating. On the other hand, each increase in family income level leads to a drop in the satisfaction rating by –0.244 units.

The *Standardized Coefficients* (*Beta*) are calculated so that you can directly compare the effects of the independent variables, since they are all measured on different scales. Notice that the beta coefficients of income and reliability rating are approximately equal, even though the *B* coefficients were not. This means that the two variables are of equal importance in predicting satisfaction.

Regression makes many assumptions about the data, which you can test using SPSS. In particular, test for the effects of multicollinearity, caused by high correlations between the independent variables.

What's Next?

This chapter concludes the discussion of the SPSS Base system statistical techniques that are useful for survey research. Chapter 10 will discuss additional useful techniques, available in the Advanced Statistics option.

10 Advanced Statistical Techniques

Thus far in this text, you've seen a variety of statistical techniques that can be used to analyze survey data. After you've mastered crosstabulation, *t* tests, and regression, what's the next best technique to try? Although every survey is somewhat unique, there are some techniques that have proved their usefulness over the years, and this chapter focuses on these. You would use some of these techniques as a companion to the analyses already discussed, while you would use others as a substitute.

Overview of Advanced Techniques

This chapter begins with a brief discussion of each advanced technique, including what it does and how it can be used to analyze survey data. The discussion is organized according to the structure of the SPSS Statistics menu so that you can easily access a procedure when you want to try it. This chapter concludes with examples of two of the most commonly used advanced procedures, Factor and Reliability.

Regression

The Regression submenu contains seven procedures, but five are highly specialized (such as 2-Stage Least Squares) or are unlikely to be used to analyze survey data (such as Nonlinear Regression).

Logistic Regression

Logistic regression is used to predict the response for a dichotomous or binary variable, using a set of predictors that can be either interval or categorical. Standard regression should not be used for this type of dependent variable. Logistic regression can be used to predict who will buy or recommend a product or service or continue as a customer, what causes some students to fail and others to succeed in school, or why some people develop a disease or condition and others do not. If you understand regression, you can understand and use logistic regression.

Loglinear

The Loglinear submenu contains three procedures, General Loglinear Analysis, Logit Loglinear Analysis, and Model Selection Loglinear Analysis. In general, loglinear analysis is used with categorical variables and is designed to model complex relationships in crosstabulations with several variables. For example, you can build a loglinear model to study the relationships among gender, age, income, region of the country, and the type of rating given to a product or service (treating the rating variable as categorical, not interval).

A loglinear model expresses the logarithm of the expected cell frequency as a linear function of certain parameters in a manner similar to that of analysis of variance. Interaction terms (*Do females with higher incomes have different opinions than males with higher incomes?*) are of particular interest in loglinear models.

One limitation of loglinear models is that the number of cases needed increases quickly as more than a few variables are included in a model. For example, five variables, each of which has five categories, will make up a model with $(5)(5)(5)(5)(5) = 3125$ cells. In addition, the interpretation of loglinear output can be complicated.

General Loglinear Analysis

General loglinear analysis fits models where there is no dependent variable. It is probably of less interest than logit and model selection loglinear analysis for most survey research applications.

Logit Loglinear Analysis

This option is used to fit models with a dependent variable. It provides the user with the most control over the model-building process.

Model Selection Loglinear Analysis

Model selection or hierarchical loglinear analysis is often used when you have a large number of potential variables and you want to determine a reduced set to test in the two more general loglinear analysis procedures.

Classify

The three techniques on the Classify submenu are used frequently to analyze survey data and are not difficult to use correctly and effectively. The K-Means Cluster and Hierarchical Cluster analysis techniques attempt to find groups of similar cases in the file; the Discriminant Analysis procedure begins with existing groups and tries to find the distinguishing characteristics of the groups.

Cluster analysis is a multivariate procedure for finding groups of similar cases in a file. Several types of variables can be used, including interval and dichotomous. Cluster analysis can be used by market researchers to identify people with similar buying habits or by banks to identify customers with similar attitudes and demographic characteristics. Cluster analysis is usually not an end in itself; instead, clusters found in the data are used in additional analyses or in marketing and sales programs.

Discriminant analysis predicts the values of a categorical dependent variable—either nominal or ordinal—with a set of categorical and interval predictors. You can, for example, predict who has bought a product once, twice, or three times or more. Banks and mortgage companies can predict who would be a good credit risk with this technique. For dichotomous dependent variables, discriminant analysis is an alternative to logistic regression.

K-Means Cluster Analysis

This technique can be used to validate cluster models found in a previous data set, such as determining whether the same clusters exist in the population from one year to the next. It can be used with any number of cases or variables.

Hierarchical Cluster Analysis

Hierarchical cluster analysis gives the user the most control over the analysis and provides more diagnostic output. It is normally the first choice for clustering applications. Because hierarchical cluster analysis requires substantial memory, you may not be able to estimate all models with this procedure.

Data Reduction

The techniques on the Data Reduction submenu are designed to simplify or reduce data to make analysis, reporting, and interpretation easier. All are recommended for analyzing survey data.

Factor Analysis

Factor analysis is designed to group variables into a smaller number of factors by looking at the correlations between the variables. Strictly speaking, factor analysis requires interval-level data, but ordinal variables are routinely used. In survey research, factor analysis is often used to determine whether a set of variables measures or is related to an underlying dimension (such as product quality, attitude toward a hospital, or feelings about politicians). A factor analysis example begins on p. 152.

Correspondence Analysis

Correspondence analysis graphically displays the relationship between the categorical variables in a two-way crosstabulation. It is an excellent technique to use when you want to present a great deal of information in one figure. It is the most useful for larger tables where relationships are harder to recognize.

Optimal Scaling

This procedure is actually a set of three techniques that can be used to accomplish different tasks.

Homogeneity analysis is somewhat like factor analysis but can handle true categorical variables. Unlike correspondence analysis, it can handle three-way and higher crosstabulations. But like correspondence analysis, it can plot the results so that multivariate relationships are visible. Again, since so much survey data is categorical, homogeneity analysis is a natural choice to do tasks like graphically depicting the relationship between gender, age, income, and attitude toward a product. However, be aware that homogeneity analysis does not discriminate between dependent and independent variables, so it will also find relationships between categories of gender and age in this same example.

Nonlinear principal components analysis reduces a set of variables into a smaller set of uncorrelated variables that retain most of the information in the original variables. In this sense, it is very similar to factor analysis (technically, principal components analysis) for data measured on any scale. Unlike factor analysis, it allows you to see relationships between the categories of two or more variables, rather than only the variables themselves. In addition to being a replacement for factor analysis, it is often used in marketing studies to examine preference data.

Nonlinear canonical correlation analysis determines how similar sets of variables are to one another. It is the most general of the three techniques and has the power to handle more than two sets of variables simultaneously.

Scale

The techniques on the Scale submenu are used quite often in survey research.

Reliability Analysis

This procedure performs analysis on a set of questions (variables) to determine whether they form an additive scale. In other words, it provides a means to simplify the analysis and reporting of survey data by showing that a group of variables, possibly identified in factor analysis, all form a scale that is a reliable measure of some general concept. The scale might measure the ease of use of a product, the customer service of a bank, or how likely someone is to remain a member of an association. A reliability analysis example begins on p. 157.

Multidimensional Scaling

The purpose of this procedure is to graphically display complex relationships by constructing a map of the location of a set of objects relative to each other. For example, multidimensional scaling can be used to take the ratings of a group of people about several products, services, or other objects and indicate the degree of similarity between the objects (not the people) via a graphic. The procedure isn't restricted to attitude questions; in an example using the distances between a set of cities in the United States as input, multidimensional scaling can construct a two-dimensional grid with the cities in their appropriate relative locations.

Multidimensional scaling can be viewed as comparable to some of the optimal scaling techniques because it provides a graphic representation of objects in multidimensional space. The position of the objects is estimated from dissimilarity, rather than similarity, data.

CHAID

This procedure is used to do segmentation modeling, useful in any situation in which your overall goal is to divide a sample into segments that differ with respect to an outcome variable. CHAID (Chi–squared Automatic Interaction Detector) was first developed for direct-mail applications but has come to be used with a wide variety of survey data. You can employ it as an alternative for crosstabulation analysis with several variables.

CHAID uses either a nominal or an ordinal variable as the outcome measure, and it normally uses categorical predictors. It divides a sample based on the categories of the best predictor of the dependent variable and then splits each of these groups into smaller subgroups based on the remaining predictor variables. The results of the segmentation are presented numerically and as an easy-to-read tree diagram.

Factor Analysis

Almost every survey includes several questions asking for a person's opinion or attitude about some general topic. For example, a hospital might ask about the perceived quality of care, a hotel might ask about the food and service in its restaurants, or a bank might ask about the quality of its loan-processing operation.

Technically, factor analysis requires an interval level of measurement, but it is commonly used on Likert scales with at least five categories.

Previous chapters have discussed how to analyze each of these questions individually and how to compare one to the other. There are methods, however, with which you can look at the questions as a group. When survey researchers ask several questions about one general topic, they have an idea—whether explicit or not—that there is an underlying factor or component that the set of questions is trying to measure. The hotel, for example, thinks that its restaurants have a general level of quality and attempts to measure it with specific questions about the food and service.

When several items potentially measure various aspects of an underlying factor or concept, you can test to determine whether the assumption that the items are related is valid. If a set of questions measures an underlying factor, the questions can be combined into a more general measure of the factor. This operation creates a more reliable measure of the factor and simplifies the description of the survey results.

Factor analysis is the statistical technique that can identify an underlying, not observable construct that is represented by a set of variables. In practice, factor analysis is often applied to many attitude items in a survey, so that more than one factor is typically discovered in a single analysis.

Requesting a Factor Analysis

To be useful, a scale should also be valid. The results of the factor analysis can be used to assess validity. Validity is harder to assess than reliability.

For this example, we'll use a different data set. A nursing care facility has conducted a survey of its residents as part of the quality improvement process. Residents were asked questions about the quality of care, buildings, food, billing, and other topics, and management wants to determine whether there are general factors for these concepts.

To request a factor analysis, from the menus choose:

Statistics
  Data Reduction ▶
    Factor...

Factor analysis has two primary steps:

- Factor extraction, which involves determining the number of factors necessary to represent the data.

- Factor rotation, which involves transforming the factors to make them more interpretable.

We've moved eight variables, all measured on a 10-point scale, into the Variables list in the Factor Analysis dialog box, as shown in Figure 10.1. The questions we're interested in concern the quality of the building and upkeep and the quality of the care provided. As with all advanced procedures, there are several pushbuttons to request additional statistics or different methods of extraction or rotation.

Figure 10.1   Factor Analysis dialog box

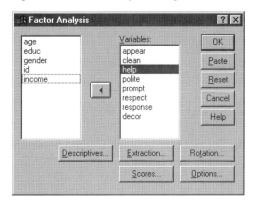

By default, Factor uses a method of extraction called **principal components**. This technique forms combinations of the variables based on the amount of explained variance (in the correlation matrix of the variables), such that the first factor explains the most variance, the second factor explains the next greatest amount of variance, and so on. This example retains the default.

Factor does no rotation by default, so you should click Rotation and choose a method. We recommend Varimax, which maximizes the explained variance.

Click Options to open the Factor Analysis Options dialog box, as shown in Figure 10.2. In the Coefficient Display Format group, you can select Sorted by size to make the output easier to read.

Figure 10.2   Factor Analysis Options dialog box

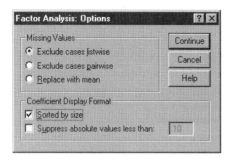

Factor analysis output has not been converted to the new Output Navigator format for release 7.0 of SPSS. Also, we present only the most crucial portions of the output here. Figure 10.3 shows the first step of factor analysis, the extraction.

Figure 10.3   Initial extraction statistics

As scales contain more items, they generally become more reliable. So, one way to increase reliability is to add more appropriate items to the scale.

```
-  -  -  -  -  -  -  -  -  -  -   F A C T O R   A N A L Y S I S   -  -  -  -  -  -  -  -  -  -  -



Analysis number 1   Listwise deletion of cases with missing values


Extraction   1 for analysis   1, Principal Components Analysis (PC)


Initial Statistics:


Variable    Communality  *  Factor   Eigenvalue   Pct of Var   Cum Pct
                         *
APPEAR        1.00000    *    1        4.21489       52.7        52.7
CLEAN         1.00000    *    2        1.26785       15.8        68.5
HELP          1.00000    *    3         .66002        8.3        76.8
POLITE        1.00000    *    4         .46466        5.8        82.6
PROMPT        1.00000    *    5         .45543        5.7        88.3
RESPECT       1.00000    *    6         .40993        5.1        93.4
RESPONSE      1.00000    *    7         .30560        3.8        97.2
DECOR         1.00000    *    8         .22162        2.8       100.0

PC    extracted   2 factors.
```

Factor will extract the first two factors, each of which explains more variance than an individual item

The most important parts of the output are the columns to the right of the asterisks. Although you can have as many factors as variables, the goal is to have only a few factors. The first two factors together explain 68.5% of the variance (52.7% and 15.8%, respectively), which is a satisfactory amount. Factor will retain only these two for the rotation phase of the procedure. Figure 10.4 shows the rotation results.

Figure 10.4   Varimax-rotated factor matrix

```
VARIMAX converged in 3 iterations.


Rotated Factor Matrix:


            Factor  1      Factor  2

POLITE        .83466         .18603
RESPECT       .81737         .00107
HELP          .78144         .35435
PROMPT        .77059         .35605
RESPONSE      .73405         .27624

DECOR         .21010         .84007
CLEAN         .26784         .77739
APPEAR        .12194         .75541
```

Each extracted factor is represented by a column. The numbers in each column are called **factor loadings** and represent the correlation between a variable and that factor. The higher the loadings (in absolute value), the more strongly a variable represents or is a component of the underlying, unmeasured factor.

The variables *polite* (politeness of staff), *respect* (respect shown by staff), *help* (helpfulness of staff), *response* (responsiveness of staff), and *prompt* (promptness of staff) load highly on the first factor. The variables *decor* (decor of the rooms), *clean* (cleanliness of rooms), and *appear* (general appearance) load highly on the second factor.

Part of the fun, and art, of factor analysis is in interpreting and labeling each factor. Factor 1 might be described as measuring the quality of care; factor 2 appears to measure the quality of the building and upkeep.

A graphic representation of this information is available if you select Loading plot(s) in the Factor Analysis Rotation dialog box. The loading plot for these two factors is shown in Figure 10.5.

Figure 10.5   Plot of the two rotated factors

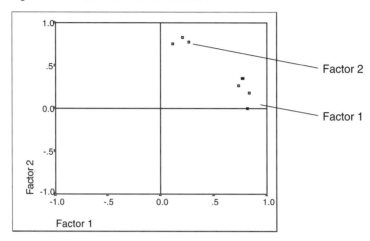

This plot has been modified by adding labels for each factor and removing the labels for each variable. The horizontal axis represents the loading on factor 1, and the vertical axis, the loading on factor 2. The position of each variable is determined by its loading on both factors. So *respect*, which falls almost on the factor 1 axis, has a factor 1 loading of approximately 0.82 and a factor 2 loading of essentially 0 (refer to Figure 10.4). The factor-loading plot shows how tightly clustered the two factors are and how distinct each is from the other.

Creating the Factors

The results of a factor analysis are never an endpoint. After determining that a set of variables is related to or representative of an underlying factor, you then can use that factor in later analyses and reports. To do this, you must combine the variables that make up the factor. Factor analysis has an option to create factor scores for each factor based on three different methods. Another frequently used option is to combine the factors by adding the scores of the variables that load highly on each factor. For example, for factor 2, you would add the scores for *appear*, *decor*, and *clean* (by using the Compute procedure).

Despite the output from factor analysis, however, it is possible that the new variable created by summing individual variables is not a *reliable* measure. To investigate this important question, we present an example of reliability analysis in the following section.

Reliability Analysis

When you want to measure a simple concept, such as age or gender, you need to ask only one question. But for complicated characteristics, such as ability in school, self-esteem, consumer attitudes about a grocery store or bank, or, in our example, attitudes about the care provided and building and upkeep in a nursing care facility, it is much better to use a set of items. Although we've used the word *scale* in earlier chapters to refer to one question measured on a Likert-type scale, another typical use of the word is to describe a measure or variable made up of several items and designed to measure a complex factor.

One natural question that arises is how well this scale does its job. There are many ways to answer such a question, but one key concept is the matter of reliability. A **reliable scale** is one that produces consistent results when given to the same individual more than once or, more relevant for survey research, produces consistent results when given to two or more persons with the same attitude toward the underlying concept.

The SPSS Reliability procedure provides a measure of the internal consistency of a scale. To request a reliability analysis, from the menus choose:

Statistics
  Scale ▶
    Reliability Analysis...

This opens the Reliability Analysis dialog box, as shown in Figure 10.6.

Figure 10.6   Reliability Analysis dialog box

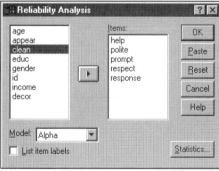

Unlike factor analysis, there are few choices to make here. For this example, we've moved the five variables that load highly on factor 1 into the Items list. Only one scale is tested at a time in Reliability, so you would have to run the procedure again to test factor 2. By default, the Alpha model will be used. In addition, we've clicked Statistics and requested all of the Descriptive statistics

(Item, Scale, and Scale if item deleted). After running the request, SPSS produces the output shown in Figure 10.7.

Figure 10.7   Item-total summary statistics and Cronbach's alpha

```
Item-total Statistics

                  Scale         Scale       Corrected
                  Mean         Variance       Item-          Alpha
                if Item       if Item         Total         if Item
                Deleted       Deleted      Correlation      Deleted

HELP           32.7180       42.1187         .7888           .8438
POLITE         32.8820       40.3768         .7673           .8503
PROMPT         32.8900       42.1582         .7658           .8495
RESPECT        32.0840       49.2675         .6334           .8795
RESPONSE       32.0100       47.8656         .6724           .8715



Reliability Coefficients

N of Cases =     500.0                  N of Items =   5

Alpha =     .8848
```

The first two columns contain the scale mean and variance if that particular item was removed from the scale. These statistics are provided because it is possible that you will want to remove items that lower the scale reliability. The third and fourth columns supply information to make that determination. The *Corrected Item-Total Correlation* is the correlation coefficient between the item and the sum of the scores for the remaining items. The lower the correlation, the less relationship there is between that item and the other items. None of the correlations is below approximately 0.63.

Cronbach's Alpha

Cronbach's alpha is derived from the average correlations of all of the items on the scale (the average covariances, in most instances). It has several possible interpretations. One that is often preferred considers alpha to represent the correlation between the items on this scale and all of the other possible scales containing the same number of items, constructed from the universe of potential questions that measure the underlying factor or concept. This sounds esoteric, but since Cronbach's alpha can be treated as a correlation coefficient, it ranges in value from 0 to 1, with higher scores indicating greater reliability. Thus, interpretation is not a difficult matter.

The value of alpha for the scale in Figure 10.7 is approximately 0.88. This is a high correlation, which means that the scale for quality of care is reliable. A guideline often used is to require alpha to be 0.70 or above, although this rule of thumb is approximate and should not be routinely applied.

The column labeled *Alpha if Item Deleted* calculates Cronbach's alpha for the scale without that item, that is, for a four-variable scale. Alpha decreases for all items, so there is no reason to drop any variables from the scale. If alpha increases when an item is deleted, you can drop that variable from the scale to increase the reliability. Of course, variables should not be dropped for only statistical reasons. If an item is important for other reasons, it should be retained on the scale unless the reliability becomes uncomfortably low.

Now that you have a reliable scale for quality of care, you can use the new variable created from summing the individual items in additional analyses and reports. Using the new variable will be more effective than working with five separate items.

Appendix
Examples of Questions and Scales

This appendix provides numerous examples of frequently used questions and response choices for a wide range of survey applications. You should feel free to experiment and adapt the examples to your own requirements, but keep in mind that many of the question formats have been successfully used by experienced survey researchers. Often, the best strategy is to use an example as is, modifying it if necessary after trying it on one or more questionnaires.

Demographics

Demographic items are more straightforward than most other question types, so the recommendations here can be more definite.

Gender

It is normally sufficient to request this information with a simple format:

Gender?   *Male* _____ *Female* _____

Or

Are you: *Male* _____ *Female* _____

Age

If you want to request age in actual years, always ask for the year of birth. The question should simply read:

Birth Year? _____

If you want to record approximate age instead, use five to six categories, such as *Under 25, 25 to 34, 35 to 44, 45 to 54, 55 to 64*, and *65 and above*. The question stem should be short.

Income

Income is almost never requested in exact dollars. The income categories you decide to use depend on whether you are surveying the general public or a more specific group. You can use up to eight categories for income (make sure they don't overlap). The most important consideration is what type of income you want to measure. Income can be defined as the respondent's income only, family income, household income, income from wages only, and so on. Following are some suggestions for phrasing family or household income questions. The word "approximate" can be added to any of these questions to indicate to the respondent that you understand his or her answer will not be exact. The word "average" can also be added so that yearly fluctuations don't affect the answer (but remember that averages are not easy to calculate).

Alternative 1   *What is your annual family income?*

Alternative 2   *What was your total family income in 1995?*

Alternative 3   *Which one of the following categories best represents your total annual family income?*

For household income:

Alternative 1   *Which of these broad categories best describes your total household income from all sources during 1995?*

Alternative 2   *What was the total income in 1995 from employment and from all other sources for all members of your household?*

Alternative 3   *What is your annual household income?*

Marital Status

If you need to record marital status, there are five generally accepted categories to use. As with gender, the question stem should be short:

Alternative 1   *Marital status?*

Alternative 2   *What is your present [current] marital status?*

The common response choices are *Never married, Married, Divorced, Widowed,* and *Separated.*

Race/Ethnicity

This question can be complex if you need to record the many variations that exist in the population. If, instead, you are satisfied with the most commonly used categories, some combination of the following is suitable:

Black [African-American], White [Caucasian], Hispanic [Latino], Asian/Pacific Islander, American Indian

If you want to be more specific since Hispanics can also be black or white, you can use these categories:

Black, Non-Hispanic; White, Non-Hispanic; Hispanic/Latino; and so on

Also, be sure to include an *Other* category. Again, keep the wording of the question short and simple.

Alternative 1   *What race do you consider yourself?*

Alternative 2   *Race?*

Alternative 3   *What is your racial/ethnic background?*

Education

Level of education is typically requested with response choices that refer to the standard levels in American education. A common set of response categories might be:

Grade school, Some high school, High school graduate, Some college, College graduate, Graduate or professional school

It is possible to use a simple question stem, as in Alternative 1:

Alternative 1   *Education level?*

But for a longer stem, you might try using this example:

Alternative 2   *What is the highest level of school you have completed?*

Labeling and Categorization

The demographic categories discussed above are the most common. To ask about those where the respondent must describe or categorize oneself, such as political party affiliation, try using these question stems:

Alternative 1   *Do you consider yourself to be a ...?*

Alternative 2   *Do you think of yourself as a ...?*

These phrasings reinforce the idea that people must place themselves in a category.

Behavior Frequency

Chapter 2 discussed some problems in measuring the frequency of behavior, mainly caused by the respondents' inaccuracy in recalling this information. Nevertheless, asking for this information is fairly common in surveys. The most important rule to follow is to always try to ask for a response in units of time that are sensibly linked to the behavior you are trying to measure. If you ask people how often they brush their teeth, don't supply response choices of *Never, Sometimes, Often,* and *Regularly.* Instead, ask people to choose from *Never, Once or twice a week, Once a day,* and *After every meal.* This second set of responses is easier to interpret and is more likely to provide accurate recall information than the first set.

However, there are times when you may have to use more ambiguous categories. In those instances, you can use variants of these response sets:

1. *Very often, Fairly often, Sometimes, Almost never, Never*

2. *Very often, Fairly often, Once in a while, Never*

3. *Often, Sometimes, Rarely, Never*

Measuring the proportion of time someone does something is slightly different. If you want to know the percentage of time a respondent buys frozen pizzas when he or she goes grocery shopping, this scale would be more appropriate:

Always, More than half the time, About half the time, Less than half the time, Seldom, Never

Attitudes

Survey researchers are most interested in questions asking for opinions, evaluations, feelings, ratings, and similar information about products, services, or organizational characteristics. Attitude questions have no right or wrong answers, unlike demographic and frequency items. So, the response categories for attitude questions will be somewhat less distinct and more difficult to interpret. In addition, the response choices you provide depend on whether you use a Likert-type scale, where only the endpoints need to be anchored, or distinct response categories (which can each be numbered).

Satisfaction

Whether you work for a hospital, bank, university, manufacturing firm, or software company, you are interested in how satisfied the respondents are with the service or product you provide. Satisfaction questions should be short, with each question asking about a single idea or concept. A typical format is to begin with this stem:

How satisfied were you with the ...

and continue with a list of items to finish the sentence. A hospital doing patient satisfaction research could use such items as:

1. Responsiveness of the nursing staff

2. Willingness of the nursing staff to provide help when it is requested

To suggest a typical list of elements to include in satisfaction questions, the following two special situations are worth exploring further.

Satisfaction for Service Organizations

Measuring satisfaction with a service (as opposed to a product) requires respondents to rate various dimensions or aspects of that service, which will vary depending on the industry. However, your questions can measure satisfaction with the following general characteristics of the service:

- Availability
- Responsiveness
- Convenience
- Quality
- Extent of knowledge
- Promptness
- Timeliness
- Friendliness
- Attention to problems
- Courtesy
- Efficiency

Employee Satisfaction

Internal surveys of employees are challenging, but following are some aspects of employee satisfaction that can be queried:

- Knowledge of policies
- Compensation plans
- Performance appraisal
- Grievance procedures
- Fair and comparable treatment
- Teamwork and cooperation

- Resolution of complaints and problems
- Health plan
- Professional development opportunities
- Organizational infrastructure (health facility, cafeteria, etc.)
- Communication
- Retirement plan
- Physical environment of work space
- Equipment/resources

Satisfaction Response Options

When using specific categories, these response alternatives are effective:

1. *Very satisfied, Satisfied, Not satisfied*

2. *Completely satisfied, Mostly satisfied, Somewhat satisfied, Mostly dissatisfied, Completely dissatisfied*

3. *Very satisfied, Slightly dissatisfied, Somewhat dissatisfied, Greatly dissatisfied*

Notice that the third alternative does not have a midpoint and uses different adjectives ("slightly" versus "somewhat") on the high and low ends. In attitude questions where Likert-type scales are not used, there is no reason to balance the scales. If you consider satisfaction to fall on a continuum from complete satisfaction to complete dissatisfaction, what is perhaps most critical is capturing this range with easily understood descriptors.

To measure satisfaction with a Likert scale, anchor the endpoints with labels of *Completely satisfied* and *Completely dissatisfied* or the equivalent.

Expectations

Whether a product or service has met someone's expectations is conceptually different from satisfaction (the latter would seem to be dependent on the former), so different response choices should be used. A typical response set is:

Below [Falls short], Meets, Exceeds

Only three categories are listed because an approximate measure of this concept is generally all that is required. Additionally, unlike satisfaction, where one cannot be more than completely satisfied, it is possible to have one's expectations exceeded, so you should allow for that.

To anchor endpoints on a scale, use *Does not meet expectations* to *Exceeds expectations*, with a midpoint of *Meets expectations*.

Ratings and Evaluations

Although satisfaction questions are common, the most frequent attitude items are those asking a respondent to rate the quality of a product or service. The wording of the question stem should generally be kept as short and simple as possible. For example, a hotel asking about the quality of its restaurants could begin with:

Please mark the answer which best describes your opinion about each characteristic.

The remainder of the question would simply list each dimension—variety of menu, quality of food, and so on—and provide response choices. Common response sets are:

1. *Excellent, Good, Fair, Poor*

2. *Excellent, Good, Average, Poor*

3. *Excellent, Very good, Good, Fair, Poor*

For any of these sets, a response of *Very poor* can be added to capture people with very low ratings, but it's usually not necessary. Of course, the use of a scale requires labeling only the endpoints with appropriate descriptors from the lists above.

When asking for a rating about the overall quality of something, think about placing the word "overall" first in the question, as in:

Overall, how would you rate the level of service provided by bank X?

Agree/Disagree

Another way to measure the rating of a product or service is to ask the respondent whether he or she agrees or disagrees with a statement about the product or service. A bank asking about the quality of service at its branches would provide declarative statements worded in a positive vein, such as:

My dealings with this branch are handled correctly the first time.

The response set is typically a Likert scale with anchored endpoints of *Strongly disagree* and *Strongly agree*, or *Completely disagree* and *Completely agree*. You can always substitute the word "totally" for "completely." If you prefer to use a set of distinct categories, consider these choices:

1. *Completely agree, Mostly agree, Agree somewhat, Completely disagree*

2. *Strongly agree, Agree, Disagree, Strongly disagree*

Problems

Problems are another measure of quality, which are different from ratings because a problem can often be measured objectively. Thus, whether or not an ATM machine is working is something that you assume would have been noticed by all customers who tried to use it that day. As noted in Chapter 2, asking about problems is most effective with response choices of *Yes* and *No*. But in terms of question wording, problems are most effectively measured with positive declarative statements. To ask about the ATM machine, the bank could begin with this stem:

The last time you used the ATM at branch X ...

and follow with these statements:

1. *The ATM area was clean.*

2. *The ATM receipt was printed correctly.*

3. *The ATM envelopes were available.*

As a general alternative to declarative sentences, you can begin with a similar stem (now asking about the employees for variety):

The last time you visited branch X ...

and follow with this type of question:

Did the employees thank you for your transaction?

Generally, the first format is more common, but you should decide which format is most appropriate for your own situation and respondents.

Comparison

To see how you stack up against your competitors, a commonly used question framework is:

How does this [product/service/organization] compare with others that you have tried [bought]?

This is an alternative when you want to compare your product, service, or organization to a series of others:

For each [product/service/organization] listed below, please indicate whether you think it is better, the same, or not as good as [name yours here].

Responses are best recorded in specific categories, for example:

1. *Much worse, Worse, About the same, Better, Much better*

2. *Better, About the same, Worse*

If you are comparing your organization's current performance to a previous time, try using only two response choices, *Better* and *Worse*, to force the respondent to make a definite evaluation.

Value/Price

Many of you are interested in whether customers believe that they have received a good value for the money they've paid for your product or service. Here are two possible questions to ask about this topic:

Alternative 1   *Would you say that product X is a good value for the money?*

Alternative 2   *Do you feel the price you paid for product X is consistent with the value of the product?*

You can use a Likert scale for response choices, or a simple *Yes/No* alternative.

Recommend

When asking whether people would recommend your product or service to others, the question can be simple, as exemplified by these examples:

Alternative 1   *Would you recommend product X to others?*

Alternative 2   *Would you recommend product X to a friend?*

Alternative 3   *How likely are you to recommend product X to others?*

If you use a Likert scale to record responses, you can anchor the ends with *Definitely would not* and *Definitely would,* or, for Alternative 3, *Not at all likely* to *Very likely.* When using specific categories, you can try:

Definitely would not, Probably would not, Probably would, Definitely would

Buy/Use Again

Asking about whether someone will use a service or buy something again can be done with this wording:

Would you use [buy] product X again [in the future]?

If you want to get a little more complex, you may find this example helpful:

If, for any reason, you had to replace your product X, do you think you would buy another from organization Z?

If you use a Likert scale for the responses, it can be anchored with one of these three sets:

1. *Definitely would not* to *Definitely would*

2. *Never* to *Definitely*

3. *Not at all likely* to *Very likely*

For labeling specific categories, a commonly used set is:

Definitely would not, Probably would not, Probably would, Definitely would

Bibliography

These references have been chosen for their clarity and comprehensiveness, and also because most are still in print. If you continue to do surveys, you may want to acquire a few to consult on a regular basis.

The references are divided into topics for ease of use. Almost all of the general references, though, contain information on most aspects of the survey process, from mode of data collection through data processing and analysis. When deciding where to look first, we recommend consulting one of the general references.

General References on Surveys

Dillman, D. A. 1978. *Mail and telephone surveys: The total design method*. New York: John Wiley and Sons.

Erdos, P. L. 1983. *Professional mail surveys*. 2nd ed. Huntington, N.Y.: R. E. Krieger.

Fowler, F. J., Jr. 1993. *Survey research methods*. 2nd ed. Newbury Park, Calif.: Sage.

Groves, R. M. 1989. *Survey errors and survey costs*. New York: John Wiley and Sons.

Mangione, T. W. 1995. *Mail surveys: Improving the quality*. Thousand Oaks, Calif.: Sage.

Rea, L. M., and R. A. Parker. 1992. *Designing and conducting survey research*. San Francisco: Jossey-Bass.

Rosenfeld, P., J. E. Edwards, and M. D. Thomas, eds. 1993. *Improving organizational surveys: New directions, methods, and applications*. Newbury Park, Calif.: Sage.

Sampling

Cohen, J. 1988. *Statistical power analysis for the social sciences*. 2nd ed. Hillsdale, N.J.: Lawrence Erlbaum.

Henry, G. T. 1990. *Practical sampling*. Newbury Park, Calif.: Sage.

Kalton, G. *Introduction to survey sampling*. Beverly Hills, Calif.: Sage.

Kraemer, H. C., and S. Thiemann. 1987. *How many subjects? Statistical power analysis in research*. Newbury Park, Calif.: Sage.

Sudman, S. 1976. *Applied sampling*. New York: Academic Press.

Writing Questions and Questionnaire Design

Converse, J. M., and S. Presser. 1986. *Survey questions: Handcrafting the standardized questionnaire.* Beverly Hills, Calif.: Sage.

Fowler, F. J., Jr. 1995. *Improving survey questions: Design and evaluation.* Thousand Oaks, Calif.: Sage.

Schuman, H., and S. Presser. 1981. *Questions and answers in attitude surveys: Experiments on question form, wording, and context.* New York: Academic Press.

Sheatsley, P. B. 1983. Questionnaire construction and item writing. In: *Handbook of Survey Research*, P. H. Rossi, J. D. Wright, and A. B. Anderson, eds. New York: Academic Press, 195–230.

Sudman, S., and N. M. Bradburn. 1982. *Asking questions: A practical guide to questionnaire design.* San Francisco: Jossey-Bass.

Sources of Questions

Bearden, W. O., R. G. Netemeyer, and M. F. Mobley. 1993. *Handbook of marketing scales: Multi-item measures for marketing and consumer behavior research.* Newbury Park, Calif.: Sage.

Davis, J. A., and T. Smith. 1991. *General Social Surveys, 1972–1991: Cumulative codebook.* Chicago: NORC.

Robinson, J. P., P. R. Shaver, and L. S. Wrightsman, eds. 1991. *Measures of personality and social psychological attitudes.* San Diego: Academic Press.

Nonresponse

Church, A. H. 1993. Estimating the effect of incentives on mail survey response rates: A meta-analysis. *Public Opinion Quarterly*, 57: 62–79.

James, J. M., and R. Bolstein. 1992. Large monetary incentives and their effect on mail survey response rates. *Public Opinion Quarterly*, 56: 442–453.

Yammarino, F. J., S. J. Skinner, and T. L. Childers. 1991. Understanding mail survey response behavior: A meta-analysis. *Public Opinion Quarterly*, 55: 613–639.

Interview Methods

Bradburn, N. M., S. Sudman, and associates. 1979. *Improving interview method and questionnaire design.* San Francisco: Jossey-Bass.

Fowler, F. J., Jr., and T. Mangione. 1989. *Standardized survey interviewing: Minimizing interviewer-related error.* Beverly Hills, Calif.: Sage.

Groves, R. M. et al., eds. 1988. *Telephone survey methodology.* New York: John Wiley and Sons.

Krueger, R. A. 1992. *Focus groups: A practical guide for applied research*. Beverly Hills, Calif.: Sage.

Lavrakas, P. 1993. *Telephone survey methods: Sampling, selection, and supervision*. Newbury Park, Calif.: Sage.

Data Processing

Bourque, L. B., and V. A. Clark. 1992. *Processing data: The survey example*. Newbury Park, Calif.: Sage.

Stouthamer-Loeber, M., and W. B. Van Kammen. 1995. *Data collection and management: A practical guide*. Thousand Oaks, Calif.: Sage.

Scale Construction

DeVellis, R. F. 1991. *Scale development: Theory and applications*. Newbury Park, Calif.: Sage.

Spector, P. E. 1992. *Summated rating scale construction: An introduction*. Newbury Park, Calif.: Sage.

Graphical Presentation

Henry, G. T. 1994. *Graphing data: Techniques for display and analysis*. Thousand Oaks, Calif.: Sage.

Kosslyn, S. M. 1994. *Elements of graphic design*. New York: W. H. Freeman.

Statistical Analysis

Bohrnstedt, G., and D. Knoke. 1994. *Statistics for social data analysis*. 3rd ed. Itasca, Ill.: F. E. Peacock.

Hays, W. L. 1988. *Statistics*. 4th ed. New York: Harcourt Brace Jovanovich.

Healey, J. F. 1993. *Statistics: A tool for social research*. 3rd. ed. Belmont, Calif.: Wadsworth.

Norusis, M. J. 1996. *SPSS 7.0 guide to data analysis*. Englewood Cliffs, N.J.: Prentice Hall.

Pagano, R. R. 1986. *Understanding statistics in the behavioral sciences*. 2nd ed. St. Paul: West.

Internet Resources

The World Wide Web contains many resources to help you do surveys and conduct data analysis. Two locations provide specific information about SPSS products and allow you to contact SPSS staff and users.

SPSS has a home page on the World Wide Web that offers information about statistics and surveys, answers to frequently asked questions about installing and running SPSS software, access to user publications, and product development information. The URL (address) for the SPSS home page is http://www.spss.com.

The SPSS Usenet news group (not sponsored by SPSS) is open to anyone interested in SPSS software products. It deals with computer, statistical, and other operational issues related to SPSS products. To subscribe, send an E-mail message to LISTSERV@UGA.CC.UGA.EDU. The text of the message should read: sub spssx-l firstname lastname.

Index